W9-CUN-447

# AUTO LEASING

*by*
Margaret C. Jasper

Oceana's Legal Almanac Series:
*Law for the Layperson*

2005
Oceana Publications
A Division of Oxford University Press, Inc.

Information contained in this work has been obtained by Oceana Publications from sources believed to be reliable. However, neither the Publisher nor its authors guarantee the accuracy or completeness of any information published herein, and neither the Publisher nor its authors shall be responsible for any errors, omissions or damages arising from the use of this information. This work is published with the understanding that the Publisher and its authors are supplying information, but are not attempting to render legal or other professional services. If such services are required, the assistance of an appropriate professional should be sought.

Library of Congress Control Number: 2005934463

ISBN 0-379-11421-6

Oceana's Legal Almanac Series: Law for the Layperson
ISSN 1075-7376

©2005 Oceana Publications, a division of Oxford University Press, Inc.

To My Husband Chris

Your love and support
are my motivation and inspiration

-and-

In memory of my son, Jimmy

# Table of Contents

## CHAPTER 3:
## THE UP-FRONT COSTS OF LEASING

## CHAPTER 4:
## THE ONGOING COSTS OF LEASING

---

CHAPTER 7:
THE FEDERAL CONSUMER LEASING ACT

## CHAPTER 8:
## DEFAULT AND REPOSSESSION

## APPENDICES

# ABOUT THE AUTHOR

MARGARET C. JASPER is an attorney engaged in the general practice of law in South Salem, New York, concentrating in the areas of personal injury and entertainment law. Ms. Jasper holds a Juris Doctor degree from Pace University School of Law, White Plains, New York, is a member of the New York and Connecticut bars, and is certified to practice before the United States District Courts for the Southern and Eastern Districts of New York, the United States Court of Appeals for the Second Circuit, and the United States Supreme Court.

Ms. Jasper has been appointed to the panel of arbitrators of the American Arbitration Association and the law guardian panel for the Family Court of the State of New York, is a member of the Association of Trial Lawyers of America, and is a New York State licensed real estate broker and member of the Westchester County Board of Realtors, operating as Jasper Real Estate, in South Salem, New York. Margaret Jasper maintains a website at http://www.JasperLawOffice.com.

Ms. Jasper is the author and general editor of the following legal almanacs: AIDS Law; The Americans with Disabilities Act; Animal Rights Law; The Law of Attachment and Garnishment; Bankruptcy Law for the Individual Debtor; Individual Bankruptcy and Restructuring; Banks and their Customers; Becoming a Citizen; Buying and Selling Your Home; The Law of Buying and Selling; The Law of Capital Punishment; The Law of Child Custody; Your Rights in a Class Action Suit; Commercial Law; Consumer Rights Law; The Law of Contracts; Co-ops and Condominiums: Your Rights and Obligations As Owner; Copyright Law; Credit Cards and the Law; The Law of Debt Collection; Dictionary of Selected Legal Terms; The Law of Dispute Resolution; Drunk Driving Law; DWI, DUI and the Law; Education Law; Elder Law; Employee Rights in the Workplace; Employment Discrimination Under Title VII; Environmental Law; Estate Planning; Everyday Legal Forms; Executors and Personal Representatives: Rights and Responsibilities; Harassment in the Workplace; Health Care and Your Rights; Hiring Household Help and Contractors: Your Rights and Obligations Under the Law; Home Mortgage Law Primer; Hospital Liability Law; How To Change Your Name; How To Protect Your Challenged Child; Identity Theft and How To Protect Yourself; Insurance Law; The Law of Immigration; International Adoption; Juvenile Justice and Children's Law; Labor Law; Landlord-Tenant Law; The Law of Libel and Slander; Living Together: Practical Legal Issues; Marriage and Divorce; The Law of Medical Malpractice; Motor Vehicle Law; The Law of No-Fault Insurance; Nursing Home Negligence; The Law of Obscenity and Pornography; Patent Law; The Law of Personal Injury; The Law of Premises Liability; Prescription Drugs; Privacy and the Internet: Your Rights and Expectations Under the Law; Probate Law; The Law of Product Liability; Real Estate Law for the Homeowner and Broker; Religion and the Law; Retirement Planning; The Right to Die; Rights of Single Parents; Law for the Small Business Owner; Small Claims Court; Social Security Law; Special Education Law; The Law of Speech and the First Amendment; Teenagers and Substance Abuse; Trademark Law; Victim's Rights Law; The Law of Violence Against Women; Welfare: Your Rights and the Law; What if it Happened to You: Violent Crimes and Victims' Rights; What if the Product Doesn't Work: Warranties & Guarantees; Workers' Compensation Law; and Your Child's Legal Rights: An Overview.

# INTRODUCTION

We live in a very mobile society, and the vehicle of choice for most people is an automobile. Acquiring that automobile is often one of the biggest and most expensive decisions a consumer can make. One must carefully consider their financial situation so that they make a decision that fits within their budget. For example, is it more affordable to lease or buy?

Leasing has become a much more common option for consumers, and there are many sources of leased vehicles, including independent leasing companies and dealerships. However, leasing doesn't fit into everyone's lifestyle. There are mileage limitations, and you are responsible for any excess wear and tear you put on the vehicle. At the end of the lease, you have to return the vehicle and, if you have to return the vehicle before the lease term ends, you may be responsible for substantial fees. Some people prefer owning their vehicle outright and not having to worry about accounting to someone for excess wear or mileage.

This almanac discusses all aspects of automobile leasing, and attempts to give the reader a basic understanding of the leasing process, and the rights and responsibilities one undertakes when leasing a vehicle. The considerations one must make in choosing to lease or buy are also discussed. The costs of leasing are explained, including up-front, ongoing and end-of-lease charges.

This almanac also discusses the laws governing leasing, including required disclosures. For example, under the federal Consumer Leasing Act, the consumer has the right to information about all of the costs and terms associated with a vehicle lease. This information helps the consumer compare lease offers. Tips on shopping for a lease, and negotiating terms are also discussed in this almanac.

The Appendix provides applicable statutes, sample forms, and other pertinent information and data. The Glossary contains definitions of many of the terms used throughout the almanac.

# CHAPTER 1:
# WHAT IS AN AUTOMOBILE LEASE?

## IN GENERAL

An automobile lease is a contract between the owner of the automobile (the "lessor") and the party who leases the automobile for his or her own use (the "lessee"), subject to the terms and limitations contained in the contract, for a specific period of time, and at a specific payment. Thus, the parties to the automobile lease are known as the lessor and the lessee. Usually, the original lessor is a dealership or an independent leasing company.

Many automobile leases are assigned to a third party at the time the lease is signed. The assignor is a lessor that sells the lease agreement and transfers the ownership rights for the leased vehicle to the assignee. The assignee is a third party that buys a lease agreement from a lessor. Once an assignment has taken place, the lessee becomes obligated to the assignee, and the assignee generally assumes the responsibilities of the lessor, although some obligations may remain with the lessor. The assignee is usually an automobile manufacturer's finance company, bank, or independent finance company.

## CONSUMER LEASE

A consumer lease is defined as a lease between a lessor and lessee for the use of personal property, that is used primarily for personal, family, or household purposes, for a period of more than 4 months, with a total contractual obligation of no more than $25,000. If the lease meets all of the foregoing requirements, it is governed by the Consumer Leasing Act and the Federal Reserve Board's Regulation M. If the lease does not meet all of these requirements—e.g., the leased property is used primarily for business and not personal purposes—the Consumer Leasing Act and Regulation M do not apply.

## TYPES OF LEASES

In order to calculate your base monthly lease payment, the end-of-term value of the vehicle must be determined. This is known as the "residual value" of the vehicle. There are publications, known as residual value guidebooks, which are used to establish vehicle residual values. The significance of the residual value depends on whether your lease is an open-end lease or a closed-end lease.

### Closed-End Lease

In a closed-end lease agreement, you are not responsible for paying the difference in value if the realized value—i.e., the actual fair market value—of your automobile at the scheduled end of the lease is less than the residual value—i.e., the projected value at lease end. You may be responsible for excess wear charges, excess mileage charges, and other lease requirements, as discussed in Chapter 5.

### Open-End Lease

An open-end lease is a lease agreement in which the amount you owe at the end of the lease term is based on the difference between the residual value of the leased automobile and its realized value. Your lease agreement will require you to pay the difference if the realized value is less than the residual value. On the other hand, you may get a refund if the realized value is greater than the residual value at the end of the lease term.

## MAINTENANCE REQUIREMENTS

When you lease a vehicle, you are required to follow all of the manufacturer's maintenance requirements. For example, you must keep the vehicle in good working order, and make any necessary repairs. The vehicle should also be serviced regularly, according to the schedule set forth in the owner's manual. Failure to properly maintain the vehicle may void any warranty or service contract you have for the vehicle.

## RELOCATION

Your lease agreement may prevent you from permanently relocating your automobile outside the state in which the lease was made. In addition, most lessors will not allow you to take the vehicle out of the country. Exceptions may be made if you are driving to Canada on a vacation trip, however, the amount of time you will be allowed to keep the vehicle out of the country will generally be limited, e.g. a maximum of 30 days.

Thus, if you are in the military, employed by a company that routinely transfers employees from state to state, or plan to retire and relocate during the term of the lease, you should carefully review any relocation restrictions contained in your lease agreement before signing. If your lease agreement does not restrict you from moving to another state, you must notify the lessor that you are moving, and properly register and title the vehicle in the new state.

If you move, you should find out how the relocation state taxes leased vehicles. Some states collect certain taxes at the beginning of the lease while other states collect those same taxes during the lease term. For example, if you paid sales and use taxes for your vehicle in your original state at the beginning of the lease, and subsequently relocate to a state that collects sales and use taxes during the lease term, you will end up paying additional sales and use taxes to the new state.

## LEASE WARRANTIES

If you like to change automobiles frequently, leasing has its advantages in terms of the warranty. The shorter the lease term you choose, the greater the likelihood that the vehicle will remain under warranty during the full lease term.

If you lease a new automobile, the vehicle would be covered under the manufacturer's warranty. If you lease a used car, the manufacturer's new car warranty may still be in effect depending on the age of the car. If the manufacturer's new car warranty is no longer in effect, and the lease agreement does not provide any other warranties, you would be taking the vehicle "as is," with no warranties as to the vehicle's condition.

If the automobile you lease has persistent problems, your state lemon law may apply. This depends on the state in which you leased the automobile. In order to find out whether you are covered by your state's lemon law, you should contact your state attorney general's office or your state office of consumer protection.

A directory of state attorney general offices is set forth at Appendix 1, and a directory of state consumer protection agencies is set forth at Appendix 2.

## TRANSFERRING YOUR LEASED AUTOMOBILE

If circumstances arise that make it impossible for you to keep your leased automobile, you may be able to transfer your lease to another person. Your right to transfer the lease is up to the lessor. There are two ways to transfer a lease to another person. First, you can keep your lease in effect and allow someone else to take possession of the car and make the lease payments. This arrangement is called a sublease. If the person takes over your lease, this is called a lease assumption.

In any event, if the lessor allows a sublease or lease assumption, the person taking possession of the car must meet all of the requirements of the lessor, including an evaluation of the person's credit history and financial background.

# CHAPTER 2:
# LEASING AND BUYING COMPARED

**SHOULD YOU LEASE OR BUY?**

The consumer must examine their financial situation to determine whether they should lease or buy an automobile. As discussed below, leasing and buying have many similarities as well as many differences. For example, leasing has a different legal structure and requires different disclosures than a loan or finance agreement to purchase a vehicle.

Leasing has become an attractive option for consumers. This is particularly so since you can get "more car for your money" with a lease as opposed to buying. There is a lower cash outlay and the monthly lease payments are usually lower than car loan payments. However, when you lease, you don't build any equity in the vehicle, you have to return it at the end of the lease, and you may have to pay extra if you exceed your mileage limitation or put excessive wear and tear on the vehicle.

When you finance an automobile, you are building equity in the vehicle and, once all of the loan payments are made, you own the car. Of course, if you pay all cash for the car when you purchase it, you own it outright from the start. However, for an identical car, monthly loan payments are generally higher than lease payments, and usually require a larger down payment.

Therefore, deciding whether to lease or buy takes careful consideration of a number of important factors. The major differences and similarities between leasing and buying an automobile are discussed below.

**OWNERSHIP**

If you lease an automobile, you do not own it. You are entitled to use it for the term of the lease, but you must return the automobile at the end of the lease unless you decide to buy it.

If you buy an automobile, you own it outright. If you finance the automobile through an installment sales contract or loan, you pay down the loan balance and eventually build equity in the vehicle. After you make your final loan payment, you acquire full ownership of the automobile.

## AVAILABILITY OF NEW AND USED AUTOMOBILES

Both new and used automobiles are generally available for leasing. The lessor may use the same lease agreement and may have some of the same policies for new and used vehicles. For example, the annual mileage allowance, the cost for excess miles, the acquisition fee, and the disposition fee may be identical. However, the maximum length of the term and the money factor may be different. The lease agreement will usually note if the vehicle is used. The current odometer reading must also be disclosed.

Both new and used automobiles are generally available for purchase and financing.

## RATE DISCLOSURE REQUIREMENT

There is no federal requirement for lessors to disclose a lease rate, and no mandatory federal formula for calculating a lease rate.

If you buy an automobile, Federal law requires disclosure of the annual percentage rate (APR). The APR is an annualized rate that reflects the total cost of credit, including interest and certain other charges. Federal law requires the use of a specific formula in calculating the APR.

## COSTS

### Up-Front Costs

The up-front costs of leasing may include the first month's lease payment; a refundable security deposit; a capitalized cost reduction—similar to a down payment; taxes; vehicle license and registration fees; a vehicle title fee; a documentation fee; and the lessor acquisition fee. You may also be offered optional insurance products and services when you lease, including credit life and disability insurance; unemployment insurance; gap coverage; vehicle maintenance services; and a vehicle service contract or mechanical breakdown protection.

If you buy an automobile, your up-front costs generally include the full cash price of the vehicle, or a down payment if you are financing the vehicle; taxes; vehicle license and registration fees; a vehicle title fee; a dealership documentation fee; and a credit application fee. As with a lease, you may also be offered optional insurance products and services, including credit life and disability insurance; unemployment insurance; gap coverage; vehicle maintenance services; and a vehicle service contract or mechanical breakdown protection.

### Refundable Security Deposit

Most leases require a security deposit at lease signing, which may be used by the lessor in case you default or at the end of the lease to offset any amounts you owe under the lease agreement.

If you buy an automobile, the financing agreement does not require a security deposit.

### Prior Lease Balance

If you lease an automobile, you are obligated to pay any balance due under a previous lease agreement after the value of the previously leased vehicle has been credited. Thus, if the lessor agrees to buy your previously leased vehicle, you will have to pay any prior lease balance unless it is included in the gross capitalized cost.

If you buy an automobile, you are obligated to pay any balance due under a previous lease agreement after the value of the previously leased vehicle has been credited. Thus, if the seller agrees to buy your previously leased vehicle, you will have to pay any prior lease balance unless it is included in the amount financed.

### Prior Credit Balance

If you lease an automobile, you are obligated to pay any amount due under a previous finance agreement after the value of the vehicle traded in on the lease has been credited. If you trade your previously financed vehicle when you lease, you will have to pay any prior credit balance unless it is included in the gross capitalized cost.

If you buy an automobile, you are obligated to pay any amount due under a previous finance agreement after the value of the vehicle traded in on the new finance agreement has been credited. If you trade your previously financed vehicle when you finance another vehicle, you will have to pay any prior credit balance unless it is included in the amount financed.

### Taxes

If you lease an automobile, you typically have to pay certain taxes when you sign the lease, depending on the taxation rules of the state and the policies of the lessor. These taxes may include: (1) State sales tax on any capitalized cost reduction; (2) County or other local taxes; (3) State sales tax on the adjusted capitalized cost; and (4) State property tax on the vehicle. Instead of paying for these taxes at lease signing, you may have the option of having the lessor include them in the gross capitalized cost, thereby increasing your monthly payment.

If you buy an automobile, you are also obligated to pay taxes. State and local sales taxes are typically assessed on the full purchase price of the vehicle. However, if a vehicle is traded as part of the purchase, sales tax may be assessed on only the purchase price minus the trade-in value, depending on state law. Several other types of taxes may be due at purchase, depending on the taxation rules of the states, including: (1) County or other local taxes; and (2) State property tax on the vehicle. You may have the option of having the creditor pay these taxes and include them in the amount financed, however, this will increase your monthly payment.

### Monthly Payments

If you lease an automobile, you pay a monthly lease payment at the beginning of each month during the term of the lease. Your first monthly payment is due at lease signing. The lessor may also require you to pay one or more of the final lease payments at signing. If you obtain a single payment lease, you make one large payment at lease signing instead of monthly payments. Monthly lease payments are usually lower than monthly loan payments because you are paying only for the vehicle's depreciation during the lease term, plus a rent charge, which is similar to loan interest, taxes, and fees.

If you buy an automobile, most finance agreements require you to make monthly payments at the end of each monthly period, thus, your first monthly payment is not made at purchase. Monthly loan payments on a vehicle purchase are usually higher than monthly lease payments because you are paying for the entire purchase price of the vehicle, less any down payment, plus interest and other finance charges, taxes, and fees. Additional charges may include service contracts, insurance, maintenance agreements, and any outstanding loan or lease balance.

### End of Term Costs

At the end of the lease term, you return the automobile and pay any end-of-lease costs, as discussed below. However, if you want to purchase the leased vehicle, or lease another vehicle, you will have additional costs.

If you buy an automobile, you do not have to return it at the end of the financing term, and there are no further loan.

### Mileage

If you lease an automobile, your contract generally limits the number of miles you may drive per year, e.g., 15,000. If you drive a lot, you can usually negotiate a higher mileage allowance in exchange for an additional payment. If you exceed the mileage limit, you will have to pay a predetermined charge—e.g., 10 to 25 cents per mile—for any excess miles.

If you buy an automobile, there is no limitation on the number of miles you drive. However, the number of miles you put on your vehicle does affect the future trade-in or resale value of the vehicle. Higher miles will reduce the vehicle's value while lesser miles will increase the trade-in or resale value.

### Wear and Tear

If you lease an automobile, your contract will generally set forth acceptable "wear and tear" limitations for the term of the lease. When you return the vehicle at the end of the lease term, if it is determined that the vehicle has more wear and tear than allowed, you will have to pay extra charges.

If you buy an automobile, there are no wear and tear limitations or charges. This is because the creditor who finances the loan, unlike the lessor, does not take any risks regarding the end-of-term value of the vehicle. It is the purchaser who suffers the consequences because excessive wear will reduce the vehicle's future trade-in or resale value.

### Early Termination Charges

If you lease an automobile, you are responsible for any early termination charges if you end the lease early. The early termination charge is typically the difference between the remaining balance on the lease and the amount credited for the realized value—i.e., fair market value—of the vehicle. This amount may be substantial, and may exceed the amount you would pay if you finished the lease term.

If you buy an automobile, you are responsible for the loan pay-off amount if you end the loan early. If you prepay your loan, you may have to pay a prepayment penalty, or you may be entitled to a refund of part of the finance charge paid. The federal Truth in Lending Act (TILA) requires the creditor to disclose whether there is a penalty or refund provision in the financing documents.

## FUTURE VALUE

If you lease an automobile, the lessor has the risk of a reduced future market value of the leased vehicle. The vehicle's future value depends on a number of factors, which cannot be known at the start of the lease term.

If you buy an automobile, you absorb any loss in the market value of the vehicle when you sell or trade it.

## DEPRECIATION

If you lease an automobile, the amount of depreciation for which you will be responsible is fixed at the beginning of the lease and stated in the lease documents.

If you buy an automobile, the amount of depreciation is unknown. Depreciation can be estimated by using guidebooks. One way to estimate depreciation when you buy a vehicle is to subtract the vehicle's estimated future value from its purchase price.

## CONDITIONS ON VEHICLE USE

If you lease an automobile, you have the right to use the vehicle for a specified period of time, subject to certain provisions contained in the lease agreement. These conditions typically include:

1. A mileage limitation;

2. Insurance requirements;

3. Maintenance and use requirements;

4. Limitations on vehicle alterations;

5. Restrictions on subleasing;

6. Limitations on drivers;

7. Restrictions designed to ensure that the vehicle will be in good operating condition at the end of the lease, including a limitation on the amount of wear and tear to the vehicle.

8. Provisions concerning your right to purchase the vehicle at the end of the lease. Most leases give you the right to purchase the vehicle at the end of the lease term. If the lease agreement gives you the right to purchase, the purchase price, or the method of determining the price, is stated in the lease agreement. If you do not have the right to purchase the vehicle at the end of the lease term, there must be a statement in the lease disclosure that there is no purchase option.

9. The duty to return the vehicle; and

10. Provisions for vehicle registration and titling, which require you to register the vehicle in the state where the vehicle is kept. However, the title to the vehicle remains in the name of the lessor or the assignee.

If you buy an automobile, the finance agreement contains conditions that protect the creditor's security interest in the vehicle until the loan is paid. These conditions typically include:

1. Insurance requirements for the vehicle;

2. Maintenance and use requirements;

3. Restrictions on renting or leasing the vehicle;

4. Provisions for early loan payment subject to any prepayment charges, which must be stated in the financing agreement;

5. Provisions for registration and titling the vehicle, which require you to list the creditor as a lien holder on the title until the loan is paid, at which time the creditor releases the lien.

## VEHICLE MAINTENANCE PROVISIONS

If you lease an automobile, you will be required to follow all of the manufacturer's maintenance requirements, including regular servicing of the vehicle and any necessary repairs. You will be responsible for any excessive wear at the end of the lease term.

If you buy an automobile, the financing agreement may also require you to follow all of the manufacturer maintenance requirements or you risk voiding the vehicle's warranty provisions. You are not responsible for excess wear at the end of the financing term, however, excessive wear does negatively impact the trade-in or resale value of the vehicle.

## ALTERING THE VEHICLE

Most lease agreements prohibit you from making any changes to the vehicle. In fact, altering the vehicle could constitute a default of the lease agreement.

If you buy an automobile, there are generally no restrictions on making changes to the vehicle.

## GAP COVERAGE REQUIREMENTS

Gap coverage is often included in a lease agreement, or available for purchase at lease signing. Gap coverage is an agreement by the lessor to cover the gap amount if your vehicle is stolen or totaled in an accident. The gap amount is usually the difference between the early termination payoff and the insured value of the car.

If you buy an automobile, Gap coverage is not usually included in the finance agreement, although it can be purchased separately.

### RELOCATION RESTRICTIONS

If you lease an automobile, the lease agreement will usually prohibit you from relocating permanently outside of the state in which you leased the vehicle. In addition, you are generally restricted from leaving the country, unless you are vacationing in Canada for a maximum of 30 days.

If you buy an automobile, the finance agreement does not usually restrict you from relocating the vehicle out of state, but most prohibit you from taking the vehicle to another country. As with a lease, there is an exception, e.g., if you plan to vacation in Canada for a maximum of 30 days.

### VEHICLE RETURN

Basically, when the lease term ends, your only obligation is to return the vehicle and pay any end-of-lease costs, as discussed in Chapter 5. One fee you may be required to pay is a disposition fee, in order to defray the lessor's expenses of preparing and selling the vehicle. You may also have the option of buying or re-leasing the vehicle.

If you buy an automobile, you become the outright owner once all of the payments are made under the financing agreement. You can sell, trade or keep the vehicle. There is no disposition fee.

# CHAPTER 3:
# THE UP-FRONT COSTS OF LEASING

## IN GENERAL

The up-front costs of leasing a vehicle are those costs which are typically paid at the time the lease agreement is signed. Up-front costs may include the first month's payment; a refundable security deposit; a capitalized cost reduction, which is similar to a down payment; registration fees; taxes; and other charges due at lease signing or delivery.

## DEALER PREPARATION FEE

Some dealerships charge a dealer preparation fee to cover the expenses of preparing the automobile for lease. Sometimes, the dealer is reimbursed by the manufacturer for the preparation costs.

## ACQUISITION FEE

The acquisition fee—also known as an administrative fee, bank fee, or assignment fee—covers a variety of administrative costs associated with the lease. This may include such costs as obtaining a credit report, preparing and checking the lease documents, verifying insurance coverage, etc. The acquisition fee may be paid up front or included in the gross capitalized cost. However, if you choose to include it in the gross capitalized cost, you will increase your monthly payment and pay added rent charges.

## CAPITALIZED COST REDUCTION

The capitalized cost reduction is the sum of any cash down payment, trade-in allowance, and rebate. It is subtracted from the gross capitalized cost, leaving the adjusted capitalized cost, i.e. the lease balance. If you pay a capitalized cost reduction, the money is not refundable.

---

A capitalized cost reduction reduces your monthly payment in two ways: (1) It reduces the amount of depreciation and any amortized amounts that you pay as part of your monthly payment; and (2) It reduces the total rent charges by decreasing the adjusted capitalized cost, thereby reducing the average lease balance over the term.

## PRIOR LEASE BALANCE

A prior lease balance is an amount due under a previous lease agreement. A prior lease balance can arise in two ways. First, if your lease is terminated early and you want to lease another vehicle, your prior lease balance is any amount due from the lease that just terminated after the value of the vehicle is credited. Second, if you end your lease at scheduled termination, your prior lease balance is any remaining amount due in connection with the earlier lease, such as excess mileage charges or personal property taxes.

A prior lease balance may be paid at lease signing, or it may be capitalized. If the prior balance is paid at lease signing, it may be labeled as either a capitalized cost reduction or a prior lease balance. If the prior lease balance is capitalized, it will be included in the gross capitalized cost and paid over the term. If you choose to capitalize the prior balance, you will increase your monthly payment and pay added rent charges.

## PRIOR CREDIT BALANCE

A prior credit balance is the amount due under a previous finance agreement for a vehicle you purchased, after the value of the vehicle traded in on the lease has been credited. Thus, if you trade your previously financed vehicle when you lease, you will have to pay any prior credit balance unless it is included in the gross capitalized cost of the lease.

For example, assume that you want to lease a vehicle but still owe $10,000 on a vehicle you have financed. If you decide to trade in this vehicle and its current value is only $9,000, the $1,000 deficiency can be paid by the lessor and collected as part of your lease in one of 4 ways:

1. You may pay the $1,000 balance as an amount due at lease signing.

2. You may include the $1,000 balance in the gross capitalized cost and pay it up front as a capitalized cost reduction.

3. You may include the $1,000 in the gross capitalized cost and pay it as part of your monthly payments over the term.

4. If you include the $1,000 in the gross capitalized cost, you may pay part of it at lease signing as a capitalized cost reduction and the rest over the term as part of your monthly payments.

## SECURITY DEPOSIT

Many leases provide that a security deposit be paid at lease signing. The security deposit is required in case you default on the lease payments. It may also be used at the end of the lease to offset any amounts you owe under the lease agreement, e.g., for excess mileage. Any remaining amount may be refunded to you at the end of the lease term; however, security deposits usually do not earn interest.

The security deposit may be any amount established by the lessor, however, it is usually calculated by rounding the first monthly payment to the next $25 or $50. Some lessors offer the option of obtaining lower rent charges and a lower monthly payment by paying a higher security deposit. Lessors may waive the security deposit for repeat customers or for those paying a higher rent charge.

## TAXES

Several types of taxes may be due at lease signing, depending on the taxation rules of the state and county in which the vehicle is garaged and the procedures of the lessor. These may include:

1. State or local sales tax on any capitalized cost reduction;

2. State or local sales tax on the adjusted capitalized cost;

3. State or local property taxes on the vehicle; and

4. County or other local taxes.

Instead of paying for these taxes at lease signing, you may have the option of having the lessor pay them and include them in the gross capitalized cost. If you choose this option, you will increase your monthly payment and pay added rent charges.

## INSURANCE

When you lease, you are generally responsible for purchasing and maintaining insurance on the vehicle until the end of the lease term. The lease agreement sets forth the required insurance coverage. Typically, the lease agreement will require you to maintain liability insurance; collision insurance; and comprehensive fire and theft insurance. The lease agreement will also set forth the minimum coverage limitations and maximum deductibles required, although you may increase the coverage limits and lower the deductible.

Before you sign your lease agreement, you will be required to show that you have obtained the proper insurance coverage for the automobile. Proof of insurance generally includes the name of the insurance company, your insurance agent, the policy number, the amount of insurance, and the dates of insurance coverage.

## OPTIONAL INSURANCE AND SERVICES

You may choose to purchase optional insurance products and other services when you lease a vehicle, including:

1. Credit life and disability insurance;

2. Unemployment insurance;

3. Gap coverage;

4. Vehicle maintenance or service contract or mechanical breakdown protection; and

5. Other services or insurance coverages.

For any products or services you choose to purchase, you may be able to buy them either from the lessor or from a third party. If you buy them from the lessor, you may have the option of including them in the gross capitalized cost rather than paying for them at lease signing. If you choose to include them in the gross capitalized cost, you will increase your monthly payment and pay added rent charges.

### Gap Insurance

Gap insurance is a plan that provides financial protection in case the leased vehicle is stolen or totaled in an accident. There are two types of Gap insurance coverage. One is a waiver by the lessor or assignee of the gap amount if the vehicle is stolen or totaled. The other is a contract by a third party to cover the gap amount.

The gap amount is generally the amount by which the early termination payoff amount exceeds the insured value of the automobile. The reason this occurs is that the leased automobile usually depreciates quicker in the earlier stages of the lease. Thus, if your vehicle is stolen or totaled at the beginning of your lease term, without Gap insurance, you could end up owing more than what your insurance carrier is willing to pay for the vehicle.

Gap insurance does not usually cover any of the up-front costs of leasing; past due amounts under the lease; the insurance deductible; excess mileage or wear charges, etc. You may also be responsible for the monthly payments until the lessor receives the insurance proceeds.

Many lease agreements include gap coverage without additional charge. However, if gap insurance is not included in your lease agreement, it can be purchased separately. Gap coverage may be denied if you are in default on any of the lease terms at the time of the loss.

## OTHER CHARGES

Several other types of charges may be assessed at lease signing, such as

1. Vehicle license and registration fees;

2. Vehicle title fee; and

3. Dealership documentation fee.

If these fees are required in your lease, you may have the option of including them in the gross capitalized cost rather than paying for them at lease signing. If you choose to include them in the gross capitalized cost, you will increase your monthly payment and pay added rent charges.

## THE FIRST MONTHLY PAYMENT

### Multiple-Payment Lease

If you obtain a multiple-payment lease, your payments are made at the beginning of each monthly lease period. For this reason, the first monthly payment is typically due at lease signing. Some leases also require that the last monthly payment or several of the final monthly payments be paid at lease signing. Most leases are multiple-payment leases.

### Single-Payment Lease

A single-payment lease is a lease agreement that requires a single large payment made in advance rather than periodic payments made over the term of the lease. Because you are making this payment in advance, this lump-sum payment should be less than the total amount you would pay in periodic payments over the term of the lease.

## PAYING UP-FRONT COSTS OVER LEASE TERM

Instead of being paid up front, many of the above costs, such as the acquisition fee, taxes, and insurance, may be capitalized—i.e., included in the gross capitalized cost and paid over the term of the lease.

If you choose to capitalize some of the costs, you will increase your monthly payment and pay added rent charges. The choice you will need to make is between: (1) higher up-front costs but lower monthly payments; and (2) lower up-front costs but higher monthly payments.

# CHAPTER 4:
# THE ONGOING COSTS OF LEASING

## IN GENERAL

The ongoing costs of an automobile lease include the monthly payments, vehicle insurance, repairs and maintenance, and registration and inspection fees. In some states, personal property taxes may also be an ongoing cost of leasing. This chapter describes these ongoing costs of leasing in more detail.

## MONTHLY PAYMENTS

If you have a multiple payment lease, you will be required to make your monthly payments in advance at the beginning of each monthly period. Monthly lease payments consists of:

(1) vehicle depreciation;

(2) amortization of any amounts included in the gross capitalized cost;

(3) rent charge;

(4) sales/use tax; and

(5) any other leasing fees.

### Vehicle Depreciation

Vehicle depreciation the amount by which a vehicle is expected to decline in value over a specific period. It is calculated as the difference between: (1) the original agreed-upon value of the automobile less any capitalized cost reduction (e.g., down payment); and (2) the residual value of the vehicle at the end of the lease (i.e., a projection of the fair market value of the vehicle at the end of the lease).

In calculating the residual value, some factors can be estimated at the time the lease is signed, such as the term of the lease and the mileage allowance. For example, if the lease is short-term, the vehicle will not be as old when it is returned, and its residual value will be higher.

A high mileage allowance will decrease the residual value because the vehicle will be expected to have more miles on its odometer when it is returned at the end of the lease term. The residual value can, therefore, be adjusted according to such factors, affect the depreciation amount, and either raise or lower the monthly payment.

You should be aware that different lessors might assign different residual values to identical automobiles with the same lease term and mileage allowance. This is because some lessors use different residual value guidelines books, and some also factor in their past experience with leased vehicles.

### Amortization of Amounts Included in Gross Capitalized Cost

Amortization of amounts included in the gross capitalized cost may include items such as taxes, fees, service contracts, insurance, and any outstanding prior credit balance or lease balance. These items are fully paid for over the term of the lease.

### Rent Charge

The rent charge is similar to the interest or finance charge on a loan. The rent charge is calculated at the beginning of the lease. It is based on the capitalized cost, the residual value, and the lease term. Unlike the interest on a loan, the rent charge is not legally required to be shown as a percentage rate, nor is there a mandatory federal formula for calculating the rent charge. The lease agreement will, however, disclose the dollar amount of the rent charge, which is included in your base monthly payment.

### Late Charges

If you fail to pay your monthly payment on time, or within the grace period provided in the lease agreement, you will likely be assessed a late charge. The late charge may be calculated as a certain dollar amount, or as a percentage of the amount of the late payment.

### Sales/Use Tax

The sales/use tax is determined by the state or county in which the automobile is registered. If the taxing authority changes the sales/use tax rate, your monthly payment could change. In most states, the monthly tax payment replaces the initial sales tax you would pay if you purchased the automobile. Some taxing jurisdictions require that the sales/use tax be paid at lease signing. In this case, you will have to pay the tax up front unless the lessor permits you to include it in the gross capitalized cost and pay it as part of the monthly payment.

### Other Lease Fees

Other lease fees may include items such as insurance; personal property tax; registration fees; and inspection fees.

### Insurance Premium Payments

As set forth in Chapter 3, you will be required to obtain insurance for your leased automobile and show proof of insurance coverage when you sign your lease. You must continue to keep this insurance coverage in effect during the lease term by paying the premium payments on a timely basis.

If you fail to keep the insurance coverage in force, you will be in default of your lease agreement. When the lessor discovers that the proper coverage is not in effect, you may be notified to secure coverage immediately to avoid repossession. If your automobile remains uninsured, the lease may be terminated, your automobile may be repossessed, and you may be liable for early termination charges. Repossession is discussed more fully in Chapter 8 of this almanac.

### Personal Property Tax

Personal property tax, also known as ad valorem tax, is based on a percentage of the automobile's value. Personal property tax is not paid at lease signing, but is due throughout the lease term. Personal property tax is usually assessed on a yearly basis. Many states do not assess a personal property tax on leased automobiles. In those states that do, you are responsible for paying the tax either to the lessor or directly to the taxing authority.

### Registration and Inspection Fees

During the lease term, you will be required to renew the vehicle registration and pay the cost of annual vehicle inspections.

## MAINTAINING YOUR LEASED AUTOMOBILE

As set forth in Chapter 1, you are responsible for maintaining your leased automobile. This means that you must have the automobile taken in for service on a regular basis, as set forth in the owner's manual. Unless the lease agreement provides that the lessor will pay for certain routine maintenance procedures, such as oil changes, you must bear the cost of all maintenance, and repairs that are not covered under any warranty.

If you fail to follow the manufacturer's guidelines, you risk voiding the warranties on the vehicle. Therefore, it is recommended that you keep copies of all of your service records, in case you need to demonstrate that you took proper care of the automobile. In addition to routine maintenance, you are also responsible for making any necessary repairs to the automobile.

## TICKETS

If you receive any tickets or fines against the leased vehicle, such as parking tickets, you must pay the tickets or fines promptly. In most states, the owner of the vehicle—i.e., the lessor—will receive notice of the tickets or fines. If the lessor pays the tickets on your behalf, you will be responsible for the amount paid and an administrative fee. In addition, non-payment of tickets and fines is usually grounds for a default on the lease.

# CHAPTER 5:
# THE END COSTS OF LEASING

## CLOSED-END LEASE

As set forth in Chapter 1, if you have a closed-end lease agreement, you are not responsible for paying the difference in value if the realized value—i.e., the actual fair market value—of your automobile at the scheduled end of the lease is less than the residual value—i.e., the projected value at lease end. Nevertheless, you are still responsible for certain charges and fees. Following are your lease-end options and the costs you are responsible for at the end of a closed-end lease term.

### Lease-End Options

At the end of your lease term, you do not own the automobile. Your lease agreement governs your options at the end of the lease. Those options may include the following.

#### Option 1: Return the Automobile

All closed-end leases offer the option of returning the vehicle at the end of the lease term to the location designated by the lessor. At that time, you will pay any amounts owed on the lease and surrender the vehicle to the lessor. End of lease charges are discussed more fully below.

#### Option 2: Extend the Lease

You may have the right to extend your lease past the lease term. You should try to negotiate a lower monthly payment for the extension period since the automobile would be considered to have a lesser value at the end of the lease term. However, if the extension is for a period of more than six months, you must be given a new set of Federal Consumer Leasing Act disclosures, as discussed in Chapter 7.

#### Option 3: Re-Lease the Automobile

You may be able to re-lease your automobile at the end of the lease term. If you do re-lease the vehicle and sign another lease, you must be given a new set of Federal Consumer Leasing Act disclosures. Again, you should negotiate a lower monthly payment for the new lease insofar as the new lease will be based on an older automobile with less value. You will also likely have to pay additional up-front costs at the beginning of the new lease term.

### Option 4: Purchase the Automobile

If your lease agreement contains a lease-end purchase option, you have the right to purchase the vehicle when the lease ends. The purchase option price and other fees and conditions are set forth in the lease agreement. Generally, the purchase option price will be stated as either (1) a fixed dollar amount, which is usually based on the residual value of the automobile; or (2) the fair market value as determined by a used car guidebook, such as the Kelly Blue Book.

Some lessors set the purchase option price as the greater of the two values. For example, if the residual value is $10,000 and the fair market value is $11,000, the purchase price would be $11,000. If the residual value is $10,000 and the fair market value is $9,000, the purchase price would be $10,000.

If you decide to purchase the automobile, you will also be responsible for title and registration fees, as well as sales tax. However, you will not be responsible for any excessive wear and tear or excess mileage charges.

### End of Lease Charges

### Final Inspection

When you schedule your return date, the automobile will be inspected for excessive wear and tear, excess mileage and any other damages to the vehicle. After the inspection is conducted, you will be given a vehicle condition report, and asked to sign it to acknowledge its receipt. If you disagree with anything in the condition report, you should note it on the form before you sign it. Your lease agreement or state law may give you the right to dispute the condition report. In order to resolve the dispute, some lessors permit you to choose a mutually acceptable third party to inspect the vehicle and issue an independent vehicle condition report. The third party condition report will then be binding on both you and the lessor.

Prior to returning your automobile for inspection, you can obtain your own independent inspection of the vehicle to determine whether it will pass the lessor's inspection. If it is determined that there is excess wear or damages, you can have the automobile repaired at the shop of your choice and have the necessary repairs made before returning the vehicle. Be aware, however, that the cost of having the vehicle repaired may exceed the charge you will pay for excess wear, and thus may not be cost effective. In any event, the vehicle repairs must meet the lessor's standards for workmanship and replacement parts. If the repairs do not meet the lessor's standards, you could still be liable for the cost of bringing the automobile up to the lessor's standards.

Once the automobile's condition is finally determined, you will be responsible for the costs of any excess mileage, excessive wear and tear, or other damage, as discussed below. These costs will be added to any other end-of-lease items you owe, such as the disposition fee, past due amounts and late charges, parking tickets, and personal property taxes, if applicable, as further discussed below.

### Disposition Fee

Depending on your lease agreement, you may be charged a disposition fee at the end of the lease term. Not all lessors charge a disposition fee. Some lessors defray these costs by charging a higher monthly lease payment. The disposition fee represents the lessor's charge for preparing and selling the automobile, and may include cleaning and reconditioning costs; inspection fees; transportation costs; storage fees; administrative fees, etc., funded by the lessor until the vehicle is sold.

### Excess Mileage Charge

Lessors assess an excess mileage charge because the residual value of the automobile is based on the expected mileage set forth in the lease agreement, e.g., 12,000 or 15,000 miles per year. The excess mileage charge generally ranges from ten to twenty-five cents per mile, depending on the type of automobile leased.

Excess miles reduces the value of the automobile. If you expect to drive more miles than the usual allotment, you should negotiate a higher mileage limit. In that case, the residual value of the automobile can be reduced to account for the higher mileage allowance. However, this will increase your monthly payment. Nevertheless, it is usually more cost-effective to negotiate the higher mileage allowance up front than to pay the excess mileage charge at the end of the lease term.

Therefore, you should carefully evaluate your driving habits to determine whether you will exceed the mileage allowance. If, during the lease term, you find out that you are driving more miles than expected, you should contact the lessor to see if you can amend the mileage allowance provision of your lease agreement. If it turns out that you do not use the extra miles you purchased, some lessors will issue a refund for the unused miles, however, the lessor's refund policy must be in the lease agreement in order to be enforceable.

### Excessive Wear and Tear Charges

Excessive wear and tear refers to wear on the automobile that exceeds the specific standards stated in your lease agreement. The standards must be reasonable. Examples of excessive wear and tear include (1) broken or missing parts; (2) dents or body damage; (3) cuts, burns or stains in the fabric or carpet; (4) excessively worn tires; (5) lack of proper vehicle maintenance; (6) broken or cracked window glass; and (7) below-standard repairs using inferior materials or parts.

The reason the lessor can charge you for exceeding the standards is because excessive wear usually decreases the value of the automobile. The residual value set forth in your lease is based on the expectation that the automobile will be returned in a certain condition. Excessive wear and tear charges may be limited by state law to the cost of actual repair, or reasonable estimates of necessary repairs. Some states resolve excess wear and tear disputes through arbitration.

For example, New York has enacted the "Motor Vehicle Retail Leasing Act" which directs the state attorney general's office to resolve "excess wear and tear" disputes through a special arbitration program, which is discussed below.

### OPEN-END LEASE

As set forth in Chapter 1, if you have an open-end lease, the amount you owe at the end of the lease term is based on the difference between the residual value—i.e., the projected value at lease end—of the leased automobile and its realized value—i.e., the actual fair market value. If there is a gain instead of a deficiency, you will receive a refund.

### Lease-End Options

As with a closed-end lease, at the end of your lease term, you do not own the automobile and your lease agreement governs your options at the end of the lease, as follows: (1) return the automobile and pay any amounts owed or receive any gain; (2) extend the lease; (3) purchase the automobile; (4) arrange for a third party to purchase the vehicle.

### End of Lease Charges

### Three-Payment Rule

In an open-end lease, as set forth above, you are responsible for any difference if the actual value of the automobile at the end of the lease term is less than the residual value stated in your lease agreement. However, assuming that you have not exceeded the mileage and wear standards, the residual value is considered unreasonable if it exceeds the realized value by more than three times the base monthly payment.

This is known as the "three-payment rule." If you believe the amount owed at the end of the lease term is unreasonable and refuse to pay, the lessor or assignee may attempt to prove that the residual value was reasonable when it was set at the beginning of the lease. However, if you cannot reach a settlement with the lessor or assignee, you cannot be forced to pay the excess amount unless the lessor or assignee brings a successful court action and pays your reasonable attorney's fees.

### Final Inspection

In an open-end lease, you are generally entitled to a refund if the realized value—actual fair market value—is greater than the residual value set forth in your lease. Therefore, the lessor may not arrange for a final inspection of the vehicle unless the lessor believes there will be a substantial deficiency. Even so, assuming there is no excess mileage or excessive wear, the lessor cannot recover any deficiency that exceeds the three-payment rule, making it highly unlikely that the lessor will bother with a final inspection.

If the lessor does arrange for a final inspection due to excessive wear and excess mileage, you should be present for the inspection and, when you receive the vehicle condition report, you can direct any questions to the person who performed the inspection.

If the lessor claims a deficiency based on the vehicle condition report, your lease agreement or state law may give you the right to dispute the condition report. As with a closed-end lease, in order to resolve the dispute, some lessors permit you to choose a mutually acceptable third party to inspect the vehicle and issue an independent vehicle condition report. The third party condition report will then be binding on both you and the lessor.

### Additional Charges

In an open-end lease, as with a closed-end lease, you may also be responsible for a disposition fee; excess mileage charges, and excessive wear and tear charges, as discussed above.

## EARLY TERMINATION

Early termination occurs when the lease term ends prematurely—i.e., before the scheduled termination date—for either a voluntary or involuntary reason. Your right to terminate your lease before the scheduled termination date is contained in your lease agreement. Some lessors permit early termination and others only permit early termination if the lessee intends to purchase the automobile.

Under the Federal Consumer Leasing Act, a lessor is required to state (1) the conditions under which a lease may be terminated early; and

(2) the amount of the early termination fee or the method for determining the early termination fee.

Typical early termination clauses contain an early termination fee, which can be substantial, e.g., thousands of dollars, although it must be reasonable under the law. The fee assessed may also include a disposition fee, late charges, parking tickets, etc.

The amount of the fee depends on the point in the lease term when you choose to terminate, e.g., the earlier you terminate, the higher the termination fee. This is because the market value of a leased automobile declines more quickly at the beginning of the lease than at the end of the lease—much quicker than the amount of your monthly payments attributable to depreciation.

Thus, the lessor must make up the difference in the depreciation payments and the actual depreciation of the automobile by charging an early termination fee. On the other hand, if you terminate the lease closer to the scheduled lease end, the opposite is true—i.e., the actual depreciation of the vehicle slows down as the amount of your monthly payments attributable to depreciation increase.

The early termination fee is usually stated as the difference between the lease payoff amount at the time of termination—e.g., the unpaid lease balance, fees and costs—and the realized value of the automobile—i.e., the credit you receive for the vehicle. For example, if you choose to return your automobile early, and the lease payoff amount at that time is $10,000, and the realized or credit amount is $9,000, you will owe a $1,000 early termination fee.

It should be noted that in an open-end lease agreement, the three-payment rule discussed above does not apply if you terminate your lease before the scheduled lease end date as set forth in the lease agreement.

### Early Termination Charge Methods

The amount of each monthly payment allocated to depreciation depends on the formula used by the lessor. Two formulas used by lessors are the (1) Constant Yield (Actuarial) Method; and (2) Rule of 78 Method.

### Constant Yield (Actuarial) Method

The Constant Yield method is the most common formula used, and refers to the method of earning rent charges in which the rent charge earned each month is proportional to the remaining lease balance. By using this method, the lessor earns rent charges at an equal rate over the term. This is similar to interest earned by a bank on a home mortgage.

### Rule of 78 Method

The Rule of 78 method refers to a method of earning rent charges in which the lessor earns rent charges faster than under the Constant Yield method so that less of each monthly payment reduces your lease balance.

Thus, if you terminate your lease early, your early termination payoff amount under the Rule of 78 method will be higher than the payoff amount under the Constant Yield method.

### Voluntary Termination

Voluntary termination occurs when you choose to end your lease before the termination date set forth in the lease agreement. Depending on your lease agreement, you may have a number of possible options if you want to get out of your lease commitment before the lease ends, as follows:

1. Return the vehicle and pay the early termination charges.

2. Trade the vehicle in to a third party. If the trade-in value exceeds your lease balance, you can keep the extra money, or you can use it towards the lease or purchase of another vehicle. If there is a deficiency, you are responsible for paying any lease balance. If you purchase another vehicle, you may be able to finance the deficiency. If you lease another vehicle, you may be able to include the deficiency amount in the gross capitalized cost of the lease.

3. If your lease agreement has an early termination purchase option, exercise the option and sell the automobile to offset any losses you sustained.

4. You can sublet the automobile and ask the lessor to substitute the new lessee as the responsible party to the lease agreement.

### Involuntary Termination

Involuntary termination occurs when the lease ends prematurely for reasons other than the lessor's choice. For example, involuntary termination occurs when the automobile is stolen or totaled in an accident, or when the lessee is in default of the lease agreement. If your vehicle is stolen or totaled, your deficiency or surplus is calculated by comparing the lease balance with the settlement proceeds from the insurance carrier. If there is a surplus, you will receive a refund. If there is a deficiency, and you have gap insurance, as discussed in Chapter 3, the deficiency amount will be reduced or eliminated.

## THE NEW YORK MOTOR VEHICLE RETAIL LEASING ACT [PERSONAL PROPERTY LAW ARTICLE 9-A §343]

The New York Motor Vehicle Retail Leasing Act (MVRLA) provides consumers with the legal right to challenge charges for excess wear and damage to the leased vehicle upon termination of their lease by participating in the New York Auto Leasing Excess Wear and Damage Arbitration Program established by the Attorney General's office.

The New York Arbitration Program enables the consumer to contest (1) whether damage to the leased vehicle exists, (2) whether such damage constitutes "excess" wear and damage, and (3) the amount of the charges sought by the lessor.

The text of the New York Motor Vehicle Retail Leasing Act [Personal Property Law Article 9-A §343] is set forth at Appendix 3.

### Covered Automobiles

The MVRLA covers new or used motor vehicles leased in New York pursuant to a retail lease agreement with a lease term of more than four months. The vehicle must be leased primarily for personal, family or household purposes.

### Wear and Damage Standard

Under the MVRLA, consumers are financially responsible for "excess wear and damage" to the leased automobile if such a provision is contained in the lease agreement. However, to hold you responsible for excess wear and damage, the law requires the lease to describe the type of damage for which you will be liable.

Excess wear and damage is commonly defined to be more than normal wear and tear, and is typically defined to include: (1) glass that is damaged or that you have tinted; (2) damaged body, fenders, metal work, lights, trim or paint; (3) missing equipment that was in or on the vehicle when delivered and has not been replaced with equipment of equal quality and design; (4) missing wheel covers, jack or wheel wrench; (5) missing or unsafe wheels or tires (including spare; snow tires are not acceptable); (6) any tire with less than 1/8 inch of tread remaining at the shallowest point; (7) torn, damaged or stained dash, floor covers, seats, headliners, upholstery, interior work, or trunk liners; (8) any mechanical damage or other condition that causes the vehicle to operate in a noisy, rough, improper, unsafe, or unlawful manner; and (9) any other damage whether or not covered by insurance.

### Notice

Under the MVRLA, the lessor must mail or deliver a notice to the consumer advising them of their rights and obligations under the law. In the case of a scheduled termination, the notice must be given not more than 40 days or less than 20 days before the end of the lease term. In the case of an early termination, the notice must be given not more than 10 business days after early termination.

The notice must advise the consumer of their right to obtain, at the consumer's own expense, before they turn in the lease vehicle, an itemized appraisal of any excess wear and damage.

### Itemized Appraisal and Bill Requirement

The lessor is required to mail an itemized appraisal and bill to the consumer by registered mail or personal delivery within 30 days after the lessor obtains possession of the vehicle. The bill must contain an itemized list of the estimated or actual cost of repairing or replacing each item, and must contain the address to which any response is to be mailed. The appraisal must be dated, signed by the lessor or its agent and identify, by type, each item of excess wear and damage. The bill and appraisal may be combined into one document.

If the consumer did not obtain an independent appraisal before turning in the automobile, they still have the right to obtain an appraisal within 10 business days after they receive the lessor's itemized appraisal and bill. The lessor must grant the consumer's licensed appraiser access to the vehicle at a reasonable time and place. The lessor is not required, however, to deliver the vehicle to the appraiser. If the lessor fails to provide reasonable access to the vehicle for the appraisal, the lessor will be deemed to have forfeited its right to collect any excess wear and damage charges.

If the lessor's claim for excess wear and damage is based on the actual cost of repairs and the consumer failed to obtain their own appraisal, they may dispute only whether any item claimed exists and/or whether such item(s) is excessive, but they cannot dispute the actual cost of the repairs.

If the consumer obtains their own appraisal and there is a discrepancy between their appraisal and the lessor's appraisal, the consumer or the lessor may submit the dispute to the lessor's informal dispute settlement procedure, if one was established.

### Right to Arbitration

Instead of submitting the dispute to the lessor's dispute settlement procedure, the consumer may instead choose to submit the dispute to the Attorney General's arbitration program. The dispute must be submitted for arbitration within 60 days from the date the lessor obtains possession of the vehicle.

If the lessor has established its own arbitration program which complies with the law's requirements, the consumer may submit their dispute to that program. However, the lessor must submit any dispute relating to excess wear and damage to its own arbitration program, if established, before pursuing any other remedy unless the consumer has opted to participate in the Attorney General's arbitration program.

The arbitration proceeding is much less complicated, time consuming and expensive than going to court. The arbitration hearing is informal and strict rules of evidence do not apply. Arbitrators, rather than judges, listen to each side, review the evidence and render a decision.

In order to participate in the arbitration program, the consumer must complete a "Request for Arbitration" form and submit it to the Attorney General's office.

The Attorney General's office reviews the form to determine whether the claim is eligible under the leasing law to be heard by an arbitrator. If accepted, the form is forwarded to the Administrator for processing. The Administrator requests the consumer to submit a filing fee and, once paid, an arbitrator is appointed and a hearing is scheduled within 35 days. If the form is rejected, it is returned to the consumer together with an explanation for the rejection.

The consumer is entitled to an oral hearing, however, the consumer can also elect to have a hearing on the documents only, unless the lessor objects. If either party fails to appear at an oral hearing, the arbitrator will nevertheless conduct the hearing and issue a decision based upon the evidence presented and any documents contained in the file.

Although the parties are entitled to hire an attorney to represent them, the arbitration program was designed to operate without the necessity of legal assistance.

The arbitrator's decision is generally issued within 10 days of the hearing. If the consumer prevails, the arbitrator's decision will provide for the refund of the consumer's filing fee. The lessor must comply with the arbitrator's decision within 30 days. If the lessor does not comply with the award, the consumer can enforce the arbitrator's decision through the courts by bringing an action to confirm the award. This action must be commenced within one year of receipt of the decision.

Either party is entitled to commence a lawsuit to challenge the arbitrator's award within 90 days of receipt of the award. However, the grounds for such challenges are limited by law. Generally, the courts will uphold an arbitrator's award if it is supported by evidence and is grounded in reason.

The New York Auto Leasing Arbitration Program Regulations are set forth at Appendix 4.

# CHAPTER 6:
# SHOPPING FOR AN AUTOMOBILE LEASE

## EXAMINE YOUR FINANCIAL SITUATION

Before you lease an automobile, you should examine your financial situation to determine whether you can afford to enter into the lease. You should have enough income and assets to take on an additional debt while maintaining your current living expenses. You should consider the advantages and disadvantages of leasing versus buying the automobile, as set forth in Chapter 2 of this almanac. It may be that financing the automobile instead of leasing is the more financially sound alternative for you.

Saving money in order to put a large down payment—known as a capital cost reduction—on the lease will result in a lower monthly payment that may fit more comfortably in your budget. A longer lease term will also result in a lower monthly payment; however, you will end up paying more money over the lease term.

When you visit the leasing company, make sure you stay within your affordable price range. Don't let the salesperson talk you into optional products if you don't want them.

## REVIEW YOUR CREDIT REPORT

In addition, you should obtain and review a copy of your credit report prior to applying for the lease. If there are any errors on the report, you should have them corrected before you apply so that you can qualify for the best rate on your lease. To obtain a copy of your credit report, contact one of the three major credit bureaus:

**Equifax Credit Information Services**

P.O. Box 740241

Atlanta, Georgia 30374

Telephone: 800-685-111

Website: www.equifax.com

**Experian**

P.O. Box 2104

Allen, Texas 75013

Telephone: 888-397-3742

Website: www.experian.com

**TransUnion Corporation**

P.O. Box 1000

Chester, Pennsylvania 19022

Telephone: 800-916-8800

Website: www.transunion.com

## COMPARE LEASE TERMS AND CONDITIONS

It is wise to research the various lease deals for the vehicle you want to lease. Compare lease rates and terms among a variety of lessors. Lease terms can vary widely among lessors. You can obtain information on leasing from automotive publications, consumer guides, articles, the Internet, advertisements, automobile dealers, and leasing companies. Some of the lease terms and conditions you should compare are set forth below.

### Monthly Payments

One of the first items to compare when shopping for a lease is the monthly payment, and the components that may affect you at the beginning or end of the lease, including the gross capitalized costs; capital cost reduction; security deposit; rent charge; and residual value.

### End of Lease Payments

Compare all of the costs you expect to have at the end of your lease term depending on whether you intend to return or purchase the automobile. For example, if you intend to return the automobile at the end of the lease term, compare the cost of the end of lease items you may incur, such as the disposition fee, excess mileage fee, excess wear and tear fee, etc.

### Gap Coverage

Some lessors charge for gap insurance while others include gap coverage in the lease without any additional charge. If gap coverage is included in the lease, compare the available coverages. If gap insurance is not included in the lease, compare the costs of purchasing gap insurance, and the coverages available.

### Rent Charge

The rent charge may vary from lease to lease. Some lessors may subsidize the rent charge and offer you a lower rent charge. Paying a lower rent charge may result in a lower monthly payment, and may reduce the lease balance faster and create a lower residual value. However, if a lease with a lower rent charge has a higher adjusted capitalized cost or a lower residual value—i.e., higher depreciation—there is no real advantage. Thus, when comparing rent charges, you need to compare the residual value, rent charge, gross capitalized cost, and the adjusted capitalized cost of the leases you are considering to determine if the lower rent charge really saves you money.

### Lease Costs

You should compare the up-front, ongoing and end-of-term costs of the lease you are considering before making a decision. You may want to minimize your up-front costs, or you may want to lower your ongoing costs.

### Total Payments

The total payments represent the overall cost of the lease. You can use this figure to compare leases. For example, although you may prefer to minimize your up-front costs, choosing a lease with lower ongoing costs may reduce the total of payments. In addition, two leases may have the same total of payments but distribute the amounts differently among the up-front, ongoing, and end-of-lease time segments. You must decide how the timing of those payments fits in your budget and your time value of money.

### Vehicle Warranty

You should compare the number of months and the mileage allowance in the lease with the vehicle's warranty period. If you are considering a lease term or a mileage allowance greater than offered by the warranty, be sure you understand what expenses you will be responsible for once the vehicle is no longer covered under the warranty.

### Purchase Option and Purchase-Option Price

Many leases offer an option to purchase the leased vehicle at the end of the lease. Your circumstances may change over the term of the lease, and having a purchase option will increase your flexibility at lease-end. When comparing leases, look to see if each offers a purchase option, what the purchase price will be, and if there is a fee to exercise the purchase option. If the vehicle turns out to have a higher market value than the residual value at the end of the lease, having a purchase option may enable you to take advantage of that difference.

### Early Termination Charges

If you end your lease early, you may face substantial early termination charges. Be sure to compare the early termination clauses in the lease agreements you are considering. There may be differences in the methods for calculating these charges

## NEGOTIATE YOUR LEASE TERMS

You don't have to accept the lease terms and conditions that are initially presented to you. You should try and negotiate your lease arrangement. Some terms and conditions are negotiable as set forth below. For those items that are not negotiable, you can shop around and compare the nonnegotiable lease terms to see if you can get a better deal for the vehicle you want to lease.

### Agreed-Upon Value of Automobile

You can negotiate the value of the automobile you intend to lease. The agreed-upon value of the automobile is the primary component of the gross capitalized cost. Thus, a lower agreed-upon value will result in lower monthly payments. When you negotiate, it is helpful to find out the lessor's cost for the vehicle. This information may be obtained through publications or through the Internet.

### Capitalized Cost Reduction

The capitalized cost reduction for a lease is similar to a down payment. Your monthly payment depends on the amount you pay up front to reduce the capitalized cost, e.g., the larger the payment, the lower your monthly payment.

### Lease Term

Most leases are for 24, 36, 48 or 60 months—i.e., 2-5 year terms. However, the duration of the lease may be negotiated. It should be noted that the longer the term of your lease, the lower the residual value will be because the vehicle will be older when it is returned at the end of the lease. This means you will end up paying more in total depreciation. If you choose to end a lease prematurely, it could be costly.

### Mileage Allowance

Annual mileage allowances for an automobile lease are usually 10,000 miles, 12,000 miles and 15,000 miles, however, you can negotiate other mileage limits. In negotiating the mileage allowance, you should try to estimate the number of miles you anticipate driving during the lease term. It is better to negotiate a higher mileage allowance if you expect to exceed the established mileage allowance to avoid paying for excess mileage at the end of the lease term. If you don't expect to drive very much, you should negotiate a lower mileage allowance. The residual value of a vehicle with high mileage is lower than the residual value of a vehicle with fewer miles.

### Options and Equipment

You are entitled to choose options and equipment for your leased automobile, such as a sunroof, global tracking system, etc. It is preferable to have those items included in the lease rather than added after you lease the vehicle. If the lessor considers the equipment as adding value for resale purposes, this will increase the residual value of the automobile. On the other hand, lessors have different policies for determining what options and equipment add value to a vehicle. Thus, adding an extra feature may not increase the vehicle's resale value.

It should be noted that some lessors will not let you add a feature or equipment to the automobile if removing it may damage the vehicle or reduce its value. In that case, you may have to surrender the accessory when you turn in the vehicle. At that time, you should be prepared to negotiate the price for any accessory that you have added to the automobile. It would be helpful to find out the lessor's cost for the particular accessory or equipment in preparation for the negotiation.

### READ THE LEASING AGREEMENT CAREFULLY

Read the leasing agreement carefully before signing to make sure all of the terms you negotiated are in writing. If it is not in writing, it is generally not enforceable. Important items to review are as follows:

1. If you negotiated the value of the vehicle, make sure the negotiated amount appears in the "agreed-upon value of the vehicle" line on the lease form.

2. If you have a trade-in, make sure the negotiated net value appears on the "net trade-in allowance" line on the lease form.

3. If you make a cash payment for the "amount due at lease signing or delivery" for the first payment, security deposit, and/or capitalized cost reduction, make sure this amount appears on the "amount to be paid in cash" line on the lease form.

4. If a rebate or discount is included in the deal, make sure this amount has been credited in the "amount due at lease signing or delivery" on the lease form.

You must make sure there are no spaces left blank in the document. If the item does not apply, either cross it our or write "N/A" in the blank space.

Make sure you understand all of the terms and conditions. If you are not sure, ask questions. Once you sign the lease agreement, both you and the lessor are obligated to abide by all of the lease terms.

The lessor is legally required to provide you with a copy of your federal lease disclosures. State laws determine whether you are entitled to copies of all the other documents that you sign. Nevertheless, you should request copies of all documents that you sign.

## GOVERNING AUTHORITIES

If you have questions about the bank or leasing company with whom you are dealing, you can contact the bank regulator or other governing authority at the addresses listed below.

### Bank Members of the Federal Reserve System

Federal Reserve Board

Division of Consumer & Community Affairs

20th & C Streets, NW – Stop 800

Washington, DC 20551

Telephone: 202-452-3693

Website: www.federalreserve.gov

### National Banks (N.A.)

Comptroller of the Currency

Office of the Ombudsman

Customer Assistance Unit

Suite 3710

Houston, TX 77010

Telephone: 800-613-6743

Website: www.occ.treas.gov

### State-Chartered Banks – Not Members of the Federal Reserve System

Federal Deposit Insurance Corporation

Compliance and Consumer Affairs

550 17th Street, NW

Washington, DC 20429

Telephone: 800-934-3342

Website: www.fdic.gov

### Federal Savings and Loan Institutions and Federal Savings Banks (FSB)

Office of Thrift Supervision

Consumer Programs/Compliance Policy

1700 G Street, NW

Washington, DC 20552

Telephone: 800-842-6929

Website: www.ots.treas.gov

### Federally Chartered Credit Unions

National Credit Union Administration

Office of Public and Congressional Affairs

1775 Duke Street

Alexandria, VA 22314

Telephone: 703-518-6330

Website: www.ncua.gov

### Captive Finance Companies, Independent Leasing Firms and Lessors Who Are Not Banks

Federal Trade Commission

Consumer Response Center

600 Pennsylvania Ave., NW

Washington, DC 20580

Telephone: 877-382-4357

Website: www.ftc.gov

## LEASE REJECTION

The lease must be signed by you and the lessor in order to be binding. However, even if both parties sign the lease, the lease agreement may contain a provision that makes the lease contingent on the lessor's ability to assign the lease to a third party. If the lessor is unable to assign the lease, you will likely receive notice from the lessor that your lease is rejected.

If this occurs, you should return to the lessor to find out why your lease was rejected. You may have other options. For example, you may be approved if you pay a larger capitalized cost reduction—i.e. down payment. You may also ask whether there are other lessors that are more likely to approve your lease on the same terms and conditions.

If these alternatives are not possible, you must cancel the lease agreement, request a refund of any money you paid at lease signing, and return the leased automobile if you already took possession of it. You should also ask for the return of your trade-in vehicle, provided you did not unconditionally sell the trade-in to the lessor. To avoid having to go through the cancellation routine, it is better to wait until your lease agreement is finally approved before surrendering your vehicle for a trade-in and taking possession of the leased vehicle.

### LEASE CANCELLATION

Generally, you do not have an automatic cancellation period after signing the lease agreement. However, if the lease agreement was signed at your home or business instead of the lessor's office, you may have a 3-day right to cancellation under federal law. State law may provide additional cancellation rights; therefore, the reader is advised to check the law of his or her jurisdiction. In addition, some lessors provide for a cancellation period in the leasing agreement.

### BUYING AND LEASING SERVICES

Some companies that offer car-buying services also provide car-leasing services. If you give the service the details about the automobile you want to lease, and your desired lease terms and conditions, these services will shop around to find you the best lease rate among a number of lessors. The service will also provide you with information that you can use to negotiate with a lessor.

### AUTOMOBILE LEASE CHECKLIST

Following is a set of questions, tips and suggestions adapted from a lease checklist published by the Federal Trade Commission designed to assist the consumer in shopping for the best lease arrangement for their financial situation.

#### Before You Shop For a Lease

##### Costs of Leasing

1. How much can you afford to pay up front?

2. How much can you afford to pay each month?

3. How much can you afford to pay at the end of the lease?

You must consider the beginning, middle, and end-of-lease costs, not just the monthly payment.

### Selecting the Vehicle

1. Have you chosen a vehicle?

2. What is the make/model/options?

Consumer guides, automotive publications, and Internet sites provide information to help you make a choice.

### Selecting a Lease Term

1. How long do you expect to keep the vehicle?

2. How long do you typically keep a vehicle?

The lease should fit your needs. Don't lease for a term longer than you intend to keep the vehicle, because you may have to pay a substantial charge for early termination. The earlier you end the lease, the greater the charge is likely to be.

### Mileage Allowance

How many miles do you usually drive a year?

Be realistic—underestimating your mileage could cost you at the end of the lease. You may want to check the odometer on your current vehicle to estimate the number of miles you typically drive.

### Purchase Option

Do you want an option in your lease to buy the vehicle?

You may want the option to buy the vehicle at the end of the lease. Keep in mind, however, that the terms of the purchase option may affect other terms in the lease.

### Insurance Coverage

1. What is your current insurance coverage for bodily injury, property damage, and liability?

2. What is your current insurance coverage for collision and comprehensive?

3. How much are your deductibles for collision?

4. How much are your deductibles for comprehensive?

Your lease may require you to carry a higher level of insurance than you currently carry. For example, the required coverage could be 100/300/50 ($100,000 of bodily injury insurance for the injuries of one person, up to $300,000 for two or more persons per accident, and up to $50,000 for property damage).

### While You're Shopping for a Lease

You should ask the following questions while you're shopping for a lease to help you evaluate and compare leases. If you're responding to an advertisement, bring the ad with you and compare the terms with other offers.

1. Vehicle year/make/model/options/equipment.

2. Lease term (number of months).

3. Mileage limit per year.

4. How much is due at lease signing—i.e., the total up-front cost?

5. How much is the capitalized cost reduction—i.e., the down payment?

6. How much are the other costs that are included in the total?

7. How much credit will you receive for any trade-in or rebates?

8. What is the agreed-upon value of the vehicle?

9. What is the gross capitalized cost of the lease? You can ask for an itemization of the gross capitalized cost, and you can usually negotiate the amount of some individual items.

10. What is the residual value of the vehicle?

11. Does the lease include an option to purchase the vehicle?

12. What is the purchase-option price, including any purchase-option fee? Fixed-price and fair-market-value purchase options may be available.

13. What is the rent charge? This amount is like the interest or finance charge on a loan or credit agreement. You may be able to negotiate this figure, but a change in the amount may affect other amounts in the lease agreement.

14. What is the total monthly payment, including taxes? Make sure the payment amount fits your budget.

15. What are the end-of-lease costs?

(a) What is the disposition fee and other end-of-lease costs? Your lease may impose a disposition fee if you do not purchase the vehicle.

(b) What is the per mile charge for any excess miles you drive?

(c) Have you reviewed the standards for excessive wear? Your lease should specify these standards.

16. Are you responsible for the maintenance costs under the lease? You are generally responsible for seeing that the maintenance requirements are met.

17. What are the insurance coverage requirements for:

(a) Bodily injury to 1 person?

(b) Bodily injury to 2 or more persons per accident?

(c) Property damage?

What are the maximum deductibles allowed by the lessor? Check with your insurance company to see what the cost of insurance coverage will be.

18. Does the lease provide gap coverage if the vehicle is totaled or stolen? If it does not, how much would gap coverage cost? Gap coverage pays the difference between the early termination payoff and the insured value of the vehicle. It does not pay for such items as insurance deductibles and past-due payments.

19. How will an early termination payoff be calculated? Different methods result in different payoff figures.

20. How much in additional fees, if any, are added to the payoff amount?

21. Have you asked about alternatives to the advertised lease? You can compare different lease offers.

22. Have you reviewed a copy of the lease? Read and understand the lease before you sign it. Make sure any oral promises are stated in the agreement.

23. Did you receive all of the required disclosures? Federal law requires that you receive important disclosures in writing before you sign a lease agreement. You should receive and keep a copy of your signed lease and any disclosures. The disclosures may be in your lease agreement or on a separate form.

### Options and Equipment

Vehicles of the same make and model will have different prices if they have different options and equipment. Use the following checklist to compare the options and equipment packages on the vehicles you are considering. Then consider any differences in options and equipment along with the differences in lease payments to determine which is the best choice for you.

1. Engine size

2. Automatic transmission

3. Air conditioning

4. Stereo tape player

5. Compact disc player

6. DVD player or other video system

7. Cruise control

8. Power windows

9. Power locks

10. Power seats

11. ABS (anti-lock) brakes

12. Sun roof/moon roof

13. Premium wheels

14. Global positioning system (GPS)

15. Mechanical breakdown protection

16. Extended warranty

17. Roadside assistance

18. Other

# CHAPTER 7:
# THE FEDERAL CONSUMER LEASING ACT

## REGULATION M

In 1976, the Truth in Lending Act was amended to include the Federal Consumer Leasing Act. Under the Federal Consumer Leasing Act, a vehicle lessor must provide the consumer with certain information before the automobile lease agreement is signed. The Federal Consumer Leasing Act is set forth at Chapter 5 of the Truth in Lending Act. Regulation M was issued by the Board of Governors of the Federal Reserve System to implement the consumer leasing provisions of the Truth in Lending Act and the Federal Consumer Leasing Act. Regulation M applies to all persons that are lessors of personal property under consumer leases, including automobile leases.

The text of Regulation M is set forth at Appendix 5.

The primary goal of Regulation M is to make sure that consumers who lease personal property receive meaningful disclosures that enable them to compare lease terms with other leases, and with credit transactions. This information is known as the Federal Consumer Leasing Act Disclosures, and is further discussed below.

A model Federal Consumer Leasing Act Disclosures form for a closed-end vehicle lease is set forth at Appendix 6.

Regulation M is also designed to provide for accurate disclosure of lease terms in advertising, as discussed below.

## DISCLOSURE REQUIREMENTS

Under the Federal Consumer Leasing Act, the required disclosures must be written clearly and conspicuously, and must be given to the consumer in a dated statement prior to the lease signing. Disclosures that are not required to be segregated may be made in either a separate dated statement that identifies the lessor, lessee and the lease transaction, or set forth in the lease agreement itself.

The required disclosures include:

1. A Description of the Property - A brief description of the leased property sufficient to identify the property to the lessee and lessor.

2. The Amount Due at Lease Signing or Delivery—The total amount to be paid prior to the lease signing, at the lease signing, or by delivery, if delivery occurs after consummation. This disclosure is required to be segregated from other information related to the lease transaction.

3. Payment Schedule—The total amount of periodic payments, including the number, amount, and due dates or periods of payments scheduled under the lease. This disclosure is required to be segregated from other information related to the lease transaction.

4. Other Charges—The total amount of other charges payable to the lessor, itemized by type and amount, that are not included in the periodic payments. Such charges include the amount of any liability the lease imposes upon the lessee at the end of the lease term. This disclosure is required to be segregated from other information related to the lease transaction.

5. Total of Payments—The total of payments, with a description such as "the amount you will have paid by the end of the lease," including:

(a) The sum of the amount due at lease signing less any refundable amounts;

(b) The total amount of periodic payments less any portion of the periodic payment paid at lease signing; and

(c) Other charges payable to the lessor.

In an open-end lease, a description such as "you will owe an additional amount if the actual value of the vehicle is less than the residual value" must accompany the disclosure. This disclosure is required to be segregated from other information related to the lease transaction.

6. Payment Calculation—A mathematical progression of how the scheduled periodic payment is derived, including the following:

(a) The gross capitalized cost;

(b) The capitalized cost reduction;

(c) The adjusted capitalized cost;

(d) The residual value;

(e) Depreciation and any amortized amounts;

(f) The rent charge;

(g) The total of base periodic payments;

(h) The lease payments:

(i) The base periodic payment;

(j) Itemization of other charges; and

(k) The total periodic payment.

This disclosure is required to be segregated from other information related to the lease transaction.

7. Early Termination Conditions—A statement of the conditions under which the lessee or lessor may terminate the lease prior to the end of the lease term; and the amount or a description of the method for determining the amount of any penalty or other charge for early termination, which must be reasonable.

8. Early Termination Notice—A notice substantially similar to the following:

"Early Termination. You may have to pay a substantial charge if you end this lease early. The charge may be up to several thousand dollars. The actual charge will depend on when the lease is terminated. The earlier you end the lease, the greater this charge is likely to be."

9. Maintenance Responsibilities—Maintenance responsibilities include:

(a) A statement of responsibilities;

(b) A statement of the lessor's standards for wear and use, which must be reasonable; and

(c) A notice regarding wear and use substantially similar to the following:

"Excessive Wear and Use. You may be charged for excessive wear based on our standards for normal use."

(d) A notice specifying the amount or method for determining any charge for excess mileage.

10. Purchase Option—A statement of whether or not the lessee has the option to purchase the leased property. If the option to purchase occurs at the end of the lease term, the purchase price must be stated. If the option to purchase occurs during the lease term, the purchase price of the method for determining the price must be stated.

11. A Non-segregated Disclosures Statement—A statement that the lessee should refer to the lease documents for additional information on items including:

(a) Early termination;

(b) Purchase options;

(c) Maintenance responsibilities;

(d) Warranties;

(e) Late and default charges;

(f) Insurance; and

(g) Any security interests, if applicable.

12. A Statement of Liability Between Residual and Realized Values—A statement of the lessee's liability, if any, at early termination or at the end of the lease term for the difference between the residual value of the leased property and its realized value.

13. Right of Appraisal—If the lessee's liability at early termination or at the end of the lease term is based on the realized value of the leased property, a statement that the lessee may obtain, at the lessee's expense, a binding professional appraisal by an independent third party of the value that could be realized at sale of the leased property.

14. A Statement of Liability at End of Lease Term Based on Residual Value.

15. Fees and Taxes—The total dollar amount for all official and license fees, registration, title, or taxes required to be paid in connection with the lease.

16. Insurance—The required disclosure must contain a brief identification of insurance in connection with the lease including:

(a) Insurance provided by or paid through the lessor, including the types and amounts of coverage and the cost to the lessee; or

(b) Insurance provided through a third party, including the types and amounts of coverage required of the lessee.

17. Warranties or Guarantees—A statement identifying all express warranties and guarantees from the manufacturer or lessor with respect to the leased property that apply to the lessee.

18. Penalties and Other Delinquency Charges—The amount or the method of determining the amount of any penalty or other charge for delinquency, default, or late payments, which must be reasonable.

19. Security Interest—A description of any security interest, other than a security deposit, and a clear identification of the property to which the security interest relates.

20. Limitations on Rate Information—If a lessor provides a percentage rate in an advertisement or in documents evidencing the lease transaction, a notice stating, "this percentage may not measure the overall cost of financing this lease" must accompany the rate disclosure. The lessor is prohibited from using the terms "annual percentage rate," "annual lease rate," or any equivalent term.

## LEASE ADVERTISEMENTS

Regulation M defines a lease advertisement as a commercial message in any medium that directly or indirectly promotes a consumer lease transaction. Under the law, a lease advertisement must comply with the following requirements:

1. Advertisements must accurately represent the products and services being offered.

2. Advertisers must adhere to fair advertising practices.

3. Advertisement disclosures must be made clearly and conspicuously.

4. If a printed ad includes any reference to the amount of any payment, a capitalized cost reduction, or other payment required at lease signing or delivery, or states that no such payments are required, then the ad must also:

(a) State that the transaction is for a lease;

(b) Set forth the total amount due at lease signing or delivery;

(c) Set forth the number, amounts, and due dates or periods of the payments; and

(d) State whether or not a security deposit is required.

5. An advertisement for an open-end lease must also include a statement that extra charges—based on the difference between the residual value and the realized value at the end of the lease term—may be imposed at the end of the lease.

### Rate Disclosure in Advertisement

The law does not require a uniform calculation and disclosure of a lease rate. There is also no mandatory federal formula for calculating a lease rate. Standardizing the lease-rate calculation would be extremely complex. It would also involve use of certain estimates that can vary among lessors. Because of certain limitations, a lease rate is not a reliable measure of the total lease cost.

## STATE LEASING LAWS

Some state laws may provide you with additional rights related to automobile leasing. States may also impose additional restrictions on lease advertising. However, a state law that is inconsistent with the provisions of the Federal Consumer Leasing Act and Regulation M is preempted to the extent of the inconsistency, unless the state law gives greater protection and benefit to the consumer.

For example, New York has enacted what it proclaims to be the strongest auto-leasing law in the country. The New York law is called the "Motor Vehicle Retail Leasing Act" and, along with the Federal Consumer Leasing Act, it provides New York consumers with strong rights when leasing a vehicle. The New York law allows consumers to shop around for the best deal when leasing a car, and sets limits on early termination charges. The New York law also directs the state attorney general's office to resolve "excess wear and tear" disputes through a special arbitration program, which is discussed in Chapter 5 of this almanac.

For further information on your state leasing laws, you should contact your state attorney general's office, or consumer protection agency.

A directory of state attorney general offices is set forth at Appendix 1 and a directory of state consumer protection agencies is set forth at Appendix 2.

# CHAPTER 8:
# DEFAULT AND REPOSSESSION

## DEFAULT

When you lease an automobile, the lease agreement gives the lessor certain rights and remedies against you in case you default on any of the provisions of the lease agreement. Therefore, it is important that you read your lease carefully to determine what acts constitute a default of the lease agreement.

For example, if you fail to pay your monthly payment on a timely basis, a typical lease agreement allows the lessor to assess a late fee, or declare you in default of the lease agreement and repossess your automobile. Obviously, the latter course of action is drastic, and most reputable lessors reserve this option for more egregious violations of the lease agreement.

If you expect that you will be unable to comply with any of the provisions of the lease agreement, e.g., you do not have the money for the monthly lease payment, you should contact the lessor to try and work out a solution instead of waiting for the lessor to seize your automobile. It is much easier to prevent the seizure from happening in the first place than to deal with the aftermath of repossession. In many cases, a lessor will work out a revised payment plan.

Nevertheless, the lease agreement does give the lessor the right to repossess the automobile if they choose to do so, and they may refuse to work out a repayment plan, or overlook a default of any of the lease agreement provisions. If the lessor takes such a strict stance, you may be able to avoid some of the costs of repossession by voluntarily agreeing to surrender the automobile. However, even if you voluntarily surrender the automobile, you will still be responsible for paying any amounts owed, including deficiency amounts, early termination fees, and other related costs.

## REPOSSESSION

In most states, the lessor can legally repossess your automobile if you are in default on the lease agreement, without having to obtain a court order, and without giving you advance notice of the repossession. Some states even allow the lessor to enter upon your property to seize the automobile. Some states have certain procedures the lessor must follow before he or she can repossess your vehicle, and if the lessor violates those procedures, they may have to pay you damages. Thus, the reader is advised to check the law of his or her jurisdiction in this regard.

Even if state law permits the lessor to seize your vehicle, the law usually prohibits the lessor from committing a "breach of peace" when carrying out the repossession. For example, some states consider seizing an automobile from a closed garage a "breach of peace," in which case the lessor may be liable to you for any damage done to your property during the seizure.

## DISPOSITION OF THE SEIZED AUTOMOBILE

Once the lessor seizes your automobile, they generally have the right to either keep it, or sell it in a public or private sale or auction. Depending on state law, the lessor may be required to notify you as to the course of action they intend to take, e.g., advise you of the time and place the vehicle will be auctioned.

If the lessor chooses to sell the automobile, the sale must be conducted in a commercially reasonable manner—i.e., according to the standards and customs of the marketplace. For example, the lessor cannot price the vehicle at the highest possible price, nor can the lessor sell the automobile for a price far below fair market value. Depending on state law, if the lessor fails to sell the automobile in a commercially reasonable manner, you may be able to sue the lessor for damages.

If your automobile is seized, the lessor is not permitted to keep or sell any personal property left in the vehicle. If personal items are missing from your automobile, you may be entitled to compensation for the loss.

## REINSTATEMENT OF THE LEASE AGREEMENT

Some states allow you to reinstate your lease agreement for the seized automobile provided you cure the breach—e.g., pay any outstanding monthly payments due on the lease—and pay all of the costs of repossession, including legal fees. However, if you subsequently cause another default of the lease agreement, your automobile can once again be repossessed and sold.

## DEFICIENCY JUDGMENT

A deficiency judgment is a court order requiring you to pay any amount you still owe on your lease agreement, after the automobile is repossessed and sold, and the proceeds applied to your unpaid lease balance. For example, if the remaining balance on your lease is $2,000, and the lessor sells your car at public auction for $1,500, the deficiency amount is $500. You are still liable for the deficiency amount, as well as any other fees owed under the lease agreement. Most states give the lessor the right to sue for the deficiency amount and all costs related to the repossession.

If the lessor sues you for the deficiency amount and related costs, you will be notified of the date you must appear in court. When you appear in court, you must be prepared to present any defense or counter-claim you may have against the lessor. For example, if the lessor breached the peace when they seized your automobile, caused damage to your personal property, or failed to sell the automobile for a commercially reasonable price, you may be able to defeat the lessor's claim for a deficiency judgment.

# APPENDIX 1:
# DIRECTORY OF STATE ATTORNEY
# GENERAL OFFICES

| STATE | TELEPHONE | ADDRESS | WEBSITE |
|-------|-----------|---------|---------|
| Alabama | 334-242-7300 | State House<br>11 S. Union St.<br>Montgomery, AL 36130 | http://www.ago.<br>state.al.us |
| Alaska | 907-465-3600 | P.O. Box 110300<br>Diamond Courthouse<br>Juneau, AK<br>99811-0300 | http://www.law.<br>state.ak.us |
| Arizona | 602-542-4266 | 1275 W. Washington<br>St.<br>Phoenix, AZ 85007 | http://www.<br>attorneygeneral.<br>state.az.us |
| Arkansas | 800-482-8982 | 200 Tower Bldg.<br>323 Center St.<br>Little Rock, AR<br>72201-2610 | http://www.ag.<br>state.ar.us |
| California | 916-445-9555 | 1300 I St.<br>Ste. 1740<br>Sacramento, CA 95814 | http://caag.state.<br>ca.us |
| Colorado | 303-866-4500 | Dept. of Law<br>1525 Sherman St.<br>Denver, CO 80203 | http://www.ago.<br>state.co.us |
| Connecticut | 860-808-5318 | 55 Elm St.<br>Hartford, CT<br>06141-0120 | http://www.cslib.<br>org/attygenl/ |
| Delaware | 302-577-8338 | Carvel State Office<br>Bldg.<br>820 N. French St.<br>Wilmington, DE 19801 | http://www.state.<br>de.us/attgen |
| District of<br>Columbia | 202-724-1305 | Office of the<br>Corporation Counsel<br>441 4th St., NW<br>Washington, DC 20001 | http://occ.dc.gov |

| STATE | TELEPHONE | ADDRESS | WEBSITE |
|---|---|---|---|
| Florida | 850-487-1963 | The Capitol PL 01 Tallahassee, FL 32399-1050 | http://myfloridalegal. com/ |
| Georgia | 404-656-3300 | 40 Capitol Square, SW Atlanta, GA 30334-1300 | http://ganet.org/ago/ |
| Hawaii | 808-586-1500 | 425 Queen St. Honolulu, HI 96813 | http://www.state. hi.us/ag/index.html |
| Idaho | 208-334-2400 | Statehouse Boise, ID 83720-1000 | http://www2.state. id.us/ag/ |
| Illinois | 312-814-3000 | James R. Thompson Ctr. 100 W. Randolph St. Chicago, IL 60601 | http://www.ag. state.il.us |
| Indiana | 317-232-6201 | Indiana Government Center South - 5th Floor 402 West Washington Street Indianapolis, IN 46204 | http://www.in. gov/attorneygeneral/ |
| Iowa | 515-281-5164 | Hoover State Office Bldg. 1305 E. Walnut Des Moines, IA 50319 | http://www. IowaAttorneyGeneral. org |
| Kansas | 785-296-2215 | 120 S.W. 10th Ave. 2nd Fl. Topeka, KS 66612-1597 | http://www.ink. org/public/ksag |
| Kentucky | 502-696-5300 | State Capitol Rm. 116 Frankfort, KY 40601 | http://www.law. state.ky.us |
| Louisiana | 225-342-7013 | Dept. of Justice P.O. Box 94095 Baton Rouge, LA 70804-4095 | http://www.ag. state.la.us/ |
| Maine | 207-626-8800 | State House Station 6 Augusta, ME 04333 | http://www.state. me.us/ag |
| Maryland | 410-576-6300 | 200 St. Paul Place Baltimore, MD 21202-2202 | http://www.oag. state.md.us |
| Massachusetts | 617-727-2200 | 1 Ashburton Place Boston, MA 02108-1698 | http://www.ago. state.ma.us |

| STATE | TELEPHONE | ADDRESS | WEBSITE |
|---|---|---|---|
| Michigan | 517-373-1110 | P.O. Box 30212<br>525 W. Ottawa St.<br>Lansing, MI<br>48909-0212 | http://www.ag.<br>state.mi.us |
| Minnesota | 651-296-3353 | State Capitol<br>Ste. 102<br>St. Paul, MN 55155 | http://www.ag.<br>state.mn.us |
| Mississippi | 601-359-3680 | Dept. of Justice<br>P.O. Box 220<br>Jackson, MS<br>39205-0220 | http://www.ago.<br>state.ms.us |
| Missouri | 573-751-3321 | Supreme Ct. Bldg.<br>207 W. High St.<br>Jefferson City, MO<br>65101 | http://www.ago.<br>state.mo.us |
| Montana | 406-444-2026 | Justice Bldg.<br>215 N. Sanders<br>Helena, MT<br>59620-1401 | http://doj.state.mt.<br>us/ |
| Nebraska | 402-471-2682 | State Capitol<br>P.O. Box 98920<br>Lincoln, NE<br>68509-8920 | http://www.nol.<br>org/home/ago |
| Nevada | 775-684-1100 | Old Supreme Ct. Bldg.<br>100 N. Carson St.<br>Carson City, NV 89701 | http://ag.state.nv.<br>us/ |
| New Hampshire | 603-271-3658 | 33 Capitol Street<br>Concord, NH<br>03301-6397 | http://www.state.<br>nh.us/nhdoj |
| New Jersey | 609-292-8740 | Richard J. Hughes<br>Justice Complex<br>25 Market St.<br>CN 080<br>Trenton, NJ 08625 | http://www.state.nj.<br>us/lps/ |
| New Mexico | 505-827-6000 | P.O. Drawer 1508<br>Sante Fe, NM<br>87504-1508 | http://www.ago.<br>state.nm.us |
| New York | 518-474-7330 | Dept. of Law<br>The Capitol, 2nd Fl.<br>Albany, NY 12224 | http://www.oag.<br>state.ny.us |
| North Carolina | 919-716-6400 | Dept. of Justice<br>P.O. Box 629<br>Raleigh, NC<br>27602-0629 | http://www.jus.<br>state.nc.us |

| STATE | TELEPHONE | ADDRESS | WEBSITE |
|---|---|---|---|
| North Dakota | 701-328-2210 | State Capitol 600 E. Boulevard Ave. Bismarck, ND 58505-0040 | http://www.ag.state.nd.us |
| Ohio | 614-466-4320 | State Office Tower 30 E. Broad St. Columbus, OH 43266-0410 | http://www.ag.state.oh.us |
| Oklahoma | 405-521-3921 | State Capitol Rm. 112 2300 N. Lincoln Blvd. Oklahoma City, OK 73105 | http://www.oag.state.ok.us |
| Oregon | 503-378-4732 | Justice Bldg. 1162 Court St. NE, Salem, OR 97301 | http://www.doj.state.or.us |
| Pennsylvania | 717-787-3391 | Strawberry Square Harrisburg, PA 17120 | http://www.attorneygeneral.gov |
| Rhode Island | 401-274-4400 | 150 S. Main St. Providence, RI 02903 | http://www.riag.state.ri.us |
| South Carolina | 803-734-4399 | Rembert C. Dennis Office Bldg. P.O. Box 11549 Columbia, SC 29211-1549 | http://www.scattorneygeneral.org |
| South Dakota | 605-773-3215 | 500 E. Capitol Pierre, SD 57501-5070 | http://www.state.sd.us/attorney/attorney.html |
| Tennessee | 615-741-5860 | 500 Charlotte Ave. Nashville, TN 37243 | http://www.attorneygeneral.state.tn.us |
| Texas | 512-463-2100 | Capitol Station P.O. Box 12548 Austin, TX 78711-2548 | http://www.oag.state.tx.us |
| Utah | 801-538-9600 | State Capitol Rm. 236 Salt Lake City, UT 84114-0810 | http://attorneygeneral.utah.gov/ |
| Vermont | 802-828-3173 | 109 State St. Montpelier, VT 05609-1001 | http://www.state.vt.us/atg |
| Virginia | 804-786-2071 | 900 E. Main St. Richmond, VA 23219 | http://www.oag.state.va.us |

| STATE | TELEPHONE | ADDRESS | WEBSITE |
|-------|-----------|---------|---------|
| Washington | 360-753-6200 | P.O. Box 40100 1125 Washington St. SE, Olympia, WA 98504-0100 | http://www.wa.gov/ago |
| West Virginia | 304-558-2021 | State Capitol 1900 Kanawha Blvd. E. Charleston, WV 25305 | http://www.state.wv.us/wvag |
| Wisconsin | 608-266-1221 | State Capitol Ste. 114 E. P.O. Box 7857 Madison, WI 53707-7857 | http://www.doj.state.wi.us |
| Wyoming | 307-777-7841 | Capitol Bldg. Cheyenne, WY 82002 | http://attorneygeneral.state.wy.us |

# APPENDIX 2:

# DIRECTORY OF STATE CONSUMER PROTECTION AGENCIES

| STATE | ADDRESS | TELEPHONE | FACSIMILE | WEBSITE |
|---|---|---|---|---|
| Alabama | Consumer Protection Division Office of the Attorney General 11 S. Union Street Montgomery, AL 36130 | 334-242-7335 | n/a | www.ago.state.al.us |
| Alaska | Consumer Protection Section Office of the Attorney General 1031 W. 4th Avenue, Suite 200 Anchorage, AK 99501 | 907-269-5100 | 907-276-8554 | www.law.state.ak.us |

| STATE | ADDRESS | TELEPHONE | FACSIMILE | WEBSITE |
|---|---|---|---|---|
| Arizona | Consumer Protection and Advocacy Section Office of the Attorney General 1275 W. Washington St. Phoenix, AZ 85007 | 602-542-3702 | 602-542-4579 | www.ag.state.az.us |
| Arkansas | Consumer Protection Division Office of the Attorney General 323 Center Street, Suite 200 Little Rock, AR 72201 | 501-682-2007 | 501-682-8118 | www.ag.state.ar.us |
| California | Department of Consumer Affairs 400 R Street., Suite 3000 Sacramento, CA 95814 | 916-445-4465 | n/a | www.dist. ct.app.ca.gov |
| Colorado | Consumer Protection Division Office of the Attorney General 1525 Sherman Street, 5th Floor Denver, CO 80203-1760 | 303-866-5167 | 303-866-5443 | www.denverda.org |
| Connecticut | Department of Consumer Protection 165 Capitol Avenue Hartford, CT 06106 | 860-713-6300 | 860-713-7239 | www.state.ct.us/dcp |
| Delaware | Fraud and Consumer Protection Division 820 N. French Street, 5th Floor Wilmington, DE 19801 | 302-577-8600 | 302-577-6499 | www.state.de.us/attgen/ |
| District of Columbia | Office of the Corporation Counsel 441 4the St. N.W., Suite 450-N Washington, DC 20001 | 202-442-9828 | 202-727-6546 | n/a |

| STATE | ADDRESS | TELEPHONE | FACSIMILE | WEBSITE |
|---|---|---|---|---|
| Florida | Economic Crimes Division Assistant Deputy Attorney General PL-01 The Capitol Tallahassee, FL 32399 | 850-414-3600 | 850-414-4483 | http://myfloridalegal.com |
| Georgia | Governor's Office of Consumer Affairs 2 Martin Luther King Jr. Drive SE Suite 356 Atlanta, GA 30334 | 404-656-3790 | 404-651-9018 | www2.state.ga.us/gaoca |
| Hawaii | Office of Consumer Protection 235 South Beretania St. Room 801 Honolulu, HI 96812-3767 | 808-586-2636 | 808-586-2640 | www.state.hi.us/dcca/ |
| Idaho | Consumer Protection Unit Attorney General's Office 650 West State St. Boise, ID 83720-0010 | 208-334-2424 | 208-334-2830 | www.state.id.us/ag |
| Illinois | Consumer Protection Division Office of the Attorney General 100 W. Randolph Street, 12th Floor Chicago, IL 60601 | 312-814-3580 | 312-814-2549 | www.ag.state.il.us |
| Indiana | Consumer Protection Division Office of the Attorney General 402 West Washington Street, 5th Fl. Indianapolis, IN 46204 | 317-232-6201 | 317-232-7979 | www.in.gov/attorneygeneral |

| STATE | ADDRESS | TELEPHONE | FACSIMILE | WEBSITE |
|---|---|---|---|---|
| Iowa | Consumer Protection Division Office of the Attorney General 1300 E. Walnut Street, 2nd Floor Des Moines, IA 50319 | 515-281-5926 | 515-281-6771 | www.IowaAttorneyGeneral.org |
| Kansas | Consumer Protection Division Office of the Attorney General 120 S.W. 10th Street, 4th Floor Topeka, KS 66612-1597 | 785-296-3751 | 785-291-3699 | www.ink.org/public/ksag |
| Kentucky | Consumer Protection Division Office of the Attorney General 1024 Capital Center Dr. Frankfort, KY 40601 | 502-696-5389 | 502-573-8317 | www.kyattorneygeneral.com/cp |
| Louisiana | Consumer Protection Section Office of the Attorney General 301 Main Street, Suite 1250 Baton Rouge, LA 70801 | 800-351-4889 | 225-342-9637 | www.ag.state.la.us |
| Maine | Consumer Mediation Service Office of the Attorney General 6 State House Station Augusta, ME 04333 | 207-626-8849 | 207-582-7699 | www.state.me.us/ag |
| Maryland | Consumer Protection Division Office of the Attorney General 200 St. Paul Place, 16th Fl. Baltimore, MD 21202-2021 | 410-528-8662 | 410-576-7040 | www.oag.state.md.us/consumer |

| STATE | ADDRESS | TELEPHONE | FACSIMILE | WEBSITE |
|---|---|---|---|---|
| Massachusetts | Consumer Protection Division<br>Office of the Attorney General<br>200 Portland Street<br>Boston, MA 02114 | 617-727-8400 | 617-727-3265 | www.ago.state.ma.us |
| Michigan | Consumer Protection Division<br>Office of the Attorney General<br>P.O. Box 30213<br>Lansing, MI 48909 | 517-373-1140 | 517-241-3771 | n/a |
| Minnesota | Consumer Services Division<br>Office of the Attorney General<br>445 Minnesota Strreet<br>St. Paul, MN 55101 | 612-296-3353 | 612-282-5801 | www.ag.state.mn.us/consumer |
| Mississippi | Consumer Protection Division<br>P.O. Box 22947<br>Jackson, MS 39225-2947 | 601-359-4230 | 601-359-4231 | www.ago.state.ms.us |
| Missouri | Consumer Protection and Trade<br>Offense Division<br>Office of the Attorney General<br>P.O. Box 899<br>Jefferson City, MO 65102 | 573-751-6887 | 573-751-7948 | www.ago.state.mo.us |
| Montana | Consumer Affairs Unit<br>1424 9th Avenue<br>Helena, MT 59620-0501 | 406-444-4312 | 406-444-2903 | n/a |

| STATE | ADDRESS | TELEPHONE | FACSIMILE | WEBSITE |
|---|---|---|---|---|
| Nebraska | Consumer Protection Division Department of Justice 2115 State Capitol P.O. Box 98920 Lincoln, NE 68509 | 402-471-2682 | 402-471-0006 | www.nol.org/home/ago |
| Nevada | Consumer Affairs Division 1850 East Sahara, Suite 101 Las Vegas, NV 89104 | 702-486-7355 | 702-486-7371 | www.fyiconsumer.org |
| New Hampshire | Consumer Protection and Antitrust Division Office of the Attorney General 33 Capitol Street Concord, NH 03301 | 603-271-3641 | 603-271-2110 | www.state.nh.us/nhdoj/consumer/cpb/html |
| New Jersey | Division of Consumer Affairs P.O. Box 45025 Newark, NJ 07101 | 973-504-6200 | n/a | www.state.nj.us/LPs/ca/home.htm |
| New Mexico | Consumer Protection Division Office of the Attorney General P.O. Box Drawer 1508 Santa Fe, NM 87504-1508 | 505-872-6060 | 505-827-6685 | www.ago.state.nm.us |
| New York | Bureau of Consumer Frauds and Protection Office of the Attorney General State Capitol, Albany, NY 12224 | 518-474-5481 | 518-474-3618 | www.oag.state.ny.us |

| STATE | ADDRESS | TELEPHONE | FACSIMILE | WEBSITE |
|---|---|---|---|---|
| North Carolina | Consumer Protection Division Office of the Attorney General P.O. Box 629 Raleigh, NC 27602 | 919-716-6000 | 919-716-6050 | www.jus.state.nc.us/cpframe.htm |
| North Dakota | Consumer Protection and Antitrust Division Office of the Attorney General 600 East Boulevard Ave. Department 125 Bismarck, ND 58505-0040 | 701-328-3404 | 701-328-2226 | www.ag.state.nd.us |
| Ohio | Consumer Protection Section Office of the Attorney General 30 E. Broad Street, 25th Floor Columbus, OH 43215-3428 | 614-466-8831 | 614-728-7583 | www.ag.state.oh.us |
| Oklahoma | Consumer Protection Unit Office of the Attorney General 445 N. Lincoln Ave. Oklahoma City, OK 73105 | 405-521-2029 | 405-5281867 | www.oag.state.ok.us |
| Oregon | Consumer Protection Section Office of the Attorney General 1162 Court St. N.E. Salem, OR 97310 | 503-378-4732 | 503-378-5017 | www.doj.state.or.us |
| Pennsylvania | Bureau of Consumer Protection Office of the Attorney General Strawberry Square, 14th Floor Harrisburg, PA 17120 | 717-787-9707 | 717-787-1190 | www.attorneygeneral.gov |

| STATE | ADDRESS | TELEPHONE | FACSIMILE | WEBSITE |
|---|---|---|---|---|
| Rhode Island | Consumer Protection Unit<br>Department of the Attorney General<br>150 South Main Street<br>Providence, RI 02903 | 401-274-4400 | 401-225-5110 | n/a |
| South Carolina | Department of Consumer Affairs<br>P.O. Box 11549<br>Columbia, SC 29211 | 803-734-3970 | 803-734-4323 | www.scattorneygeneral.org |
| South Dakota | Division of Consumer Affairs<br>Office of the Attorney General<br>500 East Capitol<br>Pierre, SD 57501-5070 | 605-773-4400 | 605-773-7163 | n/a |
| Tennessee | Division of Consumer Affairs<br>Department of Commerce &<br>Insurance<br>500 James Robertson Parkway,<br>5th Floor<br>Nashville, TN 37243-0600 | 615-741-4737 | 615-532-4994 | www.state.tn.us/consumer |
| Texas | Consumer Protection Division<br>Office of the Attorney General<br>Box 12548<br>Capitol Station<br>Austin, TX 78711 | 512-463-2185 | 512-463-8301 | www.oag.state.tx.us |
| Utah | Division of Consumer Protection<br>Department of Commerce<br>160 E. 300th Street<br>P.O. Box 146704<br>Salt Lake City, UT 84114-6704 | 801-530-6601 | 801-530-6001 | www.commerce.state.ut.us |

| STATE | ADDRESS | TELEPHONE | FACSIMILE | WEBSITE |
|---|---|---|---|---|
| Vermont | Public Protection Division<br>Office of the Attorney General<br>109 State Street<br>Montpelier, VT 05609-1001 | 802-828-5507 | n/a | www.state.vt.us/atg |
| Virginia | Consumer Litigation Section<br>Office of the Attorney General<br>900 East Main Street<br>Richmond, VA 23219 | 804-786-2116 | 804-786-0122 | www.oag.state.va.us |
| Washington | Consumer Resource Center<br>900 Fourth Avenue, Suite 2000<br>Seattle, WA 98164-1012 | 206-464-6684 | 206-464-6451 | www.wa.gov/ago |
| West Virginia | Consumer Protection Division<br>Office of the Attorney General<br>812 Quarrier Street<br>6th Floor, Charleston, WV 25326 | 304-558-8986 | 304-558-0184 | www.state.wv.us/wvag |
| Wisconsin | Division of Trade and<br>Consumer Protection<br>2811 Agriculture Drive<br>P.O. Box 8911<br>Madison, WI 53708 | 608-224-4953 | 608-224-4939 | www.datcp.state.wi.us |
| Wyoming | Consumer Protection Unit<br>Office of the Attorney General<br>123 State Capitol Building<br>Cheyenne, WY 82002 | 307-777-7874 | 307-777-7956 | agwebmaster@state.wy.us,<br>attorneygeneral.state.wy.us |

# APPENDIX 3:
# THE NEW YORK MOTOR VEHICLE RETAIL LEASING ACT [PERSONAL PROPERTY LAW ARTICLE 9-A §343]

1. (a) Upon the scheduled termination of a retail lease agreement, the lessor shall not charge, receive or collect a charge for excess wear and damage to the vehicle which exceeds: (i) the actual cost of repairs, reduced by all discounts, paid by the lessor; or (ii) a true itemized estimate of the cost of such repairs by an appraiser licensed pursuant to section three hundred ninety-eight-d of the vehicle and traffic law selected by the lessor, of the cost of such repairs.

1. (b) Upon early termination of a retail lease agreement, the lessor shall not charge, receive or collect a charge for excess wear and damage to the vehicle which exceeds the actual cost of repairs, reduced by all discounts, paid by the lessor.

2. In order for a lessor to impose a charge for excess wear and damage to a vehicle subject to a retail lease agreement, such agreement shall contain a clause describing the excess wear and damage to the vehicle for which the lessee may be liable. Such lessor shall, not more than forty days nor less than twenty days prior to the scheduled termination date, or, not more than ten business days after the date of an early termination of a lease agreement, mail or deliver to the lessee a notice advising the lessee of the following rights and obligations of the parties, herein granted and imposed:

(a) Such notice shall include the following statement, as set forth herein, at the beginning of the notice in at least ten-point bold type:

"YOUR LEASE AGREEMENT ALLOWS (LESSOR) TO ASSESS A CHARGE FOR EXCESS WEAR AND DAMAGE TO THE VEHICLE. YOU SHOULD OBTAIN YOUR OWN EVIDENCE OF THE CURRENT CONDITION OF THE VEHICLE NOT MORE THAN TWENTY (20) DAYS PRIOR TO THE SCHEDULED TERMINATION OF YOUR LEASE. YOU ALSO WILL HAVE THE RIGHT TO SUBMIT DISPUTES

TO THE ALTERNATE ARBITRATION MECHANISM ESTABLISHED UNDER REGULATIONS PROMULGATED BY THE NEW YORK STATE ATTORNEY GENERAL."

(b) In the case of a scheduled termination, of the lessee's right to turn the vehicle in with a copy of an itemized appraisal of excess wear and damage to the vehicle prepared by an appraiser licensed under section three hundred ninety-eight-d of the vehicle and traffic law, selected by the lessee and conducted not more than twenty days prior to the scheduled termination date;

(c) Of the right of the lessor to, within thirty days after the date on which the vehicle comes into the actual physical possession of the lessor, obtain a written itemized appraisal of excess wear and damage to the vehicle prepared by an appraiser licensed under section three hundred ninety-eight-d of the vehicle and traffic law selected by the lessor;

(d) That if the lessee had not previously obtained and submitted to the lessor a written itemized appraisal on the lessee's own behalf in accordance with paragraph (b) of this subdivision, the lessee will have the greater of ten business days after the lessee has received or fourteen business days to do so after the lessor has sent, in conformance with subdivision three of this section, an itemized bill for excess wear and damage and a copy of the itemized appraisal prepared on behalf of the lessor, unless the lessee does not dispute any of the items contained therein. In the case where the lessor bases the charge for excess wear and damage on the actual cost of repairs, the notice shall also inform the lessee that should the lessee fail to obtain an itemized written appraisal, he or she is entitled to dispute only whether any items claimed exist and/or are excess wear and damage to the vehicle, but not the actual cost of making the repairs;

(e) That if the lessee disputes any of the items claimed for excess wear and damage to the vehicle exist or are excessive in nature, the lessee may submit the dispute within sixty days of the date on which the vehicle comes into actual physical possession of the lessor to the lessor's informal dispute settlement procedure, if any, or, upon the payment of the prescribed filing fee which is refundable if the arbitrator finds in the lessee's favor, to an alternative arbitration mechanism established under regulations promulgated by the attorney general of the state of New York;

(f) That if there exists a discrepancy between the itemized appraisals obtained by the lessor and the lessee, if any, the lessor shall submit the dispute within sixty days of the date on which the vehicle comes into the actual physical possession of the lessor to the lessor's informal dispute settlement procedure, if any, unless the lessee exercises the option granted by paragraph (b) of subdivision five of this section; provided, however, that in the event the lessor has complied with the provisions of this subdivision, a lessee who has failed to obtain an itemized appraisal of the excessive wear and damage to the vehicle in accordance with either paragraph (b) or (c) of this subdivision may dispute only the existence of any item or whether the wear is excessive in nature, but may not dispute the actual cost of repairs.

3. (a) Itemized bill.

(i) In the event that the lessor wishes to impose a charge for excess wear and damage to the vehicle, the lessor shall send by registered mail or hand-deliver to the lessee a bill containing an itemized list of the estimated or actual cost of repairing or replacing each item as to which an excess wear and damage charge is claimed and specifying the address to which any response must be mailed. The bill shall be mailed or hand-delivered to the lessee within thirty days after the date on which the vehicle comes into the actual possession of the lessor.

(ii) The itemized bill shall include the following statements printed in at least ten-point type: "You are being asked to pay an amount claimed for excess wear and damage to the vehicle. If you wish to contest this amount, you must obtain an itemized appraisal from an appraiser licensed by the New York State Department of Motor Vehicles, and mail or deliver a copy of such appraisal to (NAME AND ADDRESS OF LESSOR) within the greater of fourteen business days after (NAME OF LESSOR) has sent, or ten business days of receipt of this bill and (NAME OF LESSOR'S) itemized appraisal. If you fail to do so, you will forfeit your right to contest in arbitration any actual repair costs incurred by the (LESSOR) for excess wear and damage; however, you do not forfeit your right to contest the existence of any item or whether the wear is excessive in nature."

(iii) The following bill shall also notify lessees of their material rights and obligations for dispute resolution in arbitration.

3. (b) Itemized appraisal.

(i) A lessor who imposes a charge for excess wear and damage to the vehicle shall send by registered mail or hand-deliver, within thirty days after the date on which the vehicle comes into actual physical possession of the lessor, a written itemized appraisal prepared by an appraiser licensed under section three hundred ninety-eight-d of the vehicle and traffic law. The appraisal shall be dated, signed by the lessor or its agent, and identify by type each item of excess wear and damage.

(ii) The following notice shall be included at the beginning of the itemized appraisal prepared on behalf of the lessor and furnished to the lessee,

"ALL ITEMS OF DAMAGE FOR WHICH A CHARGE FOR EX-CESSIVE WEAR OR DAMAGE WILL BE CLAIMED BY THE LES-SOR MUST BE NOTED IN THIS APPRAISAL. IF YOU DIS-PUTE THE EXISTENCE OR NATURE OF ANY ITEM OF DAMAGE IDENTIFIED IN THIS NOTICE, YOU MAY SUBMIT THE DISPUTE TO THE AL-TERNATE ARBITRATION MECHANISM ESTABLISHED UNDER REGULATIONS PROMULGATED BY THE NEW YORK STATE ATTORNEY GENERAL."

4. (a) The itemized bill and appraisal required by subdivision three of this section may be combined into a single document. Mere acknowledgement by the lessee of receipt of an itemized bill, an appraisal, or a combination of the two shall not operate as an admission of the existence, nature or amount of any of the items therein.

4. (b)(i) The lessor shall grant the lessee access to the vehicle at a reasonable time and place in order for the lessee to obtain an itemized appraisal on the lessee's own behalf. The lessor shall not be required, however, to deliver the vehicle to, or produce the vehicle at, a destination designated by the lessee for such purpose.

(ii) A lessor may not fail to provide, either intentionally or by actions or omissions, reasonable access to the vehicle by the licensed appraiser chosen by the lessee within the period during which a lessee must obtain and submit an appraisal. If the lessor fails to so provide reasonable access to the vehicle, the lessor shall be deemed to have forfeited its contractual right to charge, receive or collect any charge for excessive wear and damage to the vehicle from the lessee.

4. (c) A lessor or lessor of a retail lease agreement shall not report an unsatisfied claim for excess wear and damage to a credit reporting agency as a derogatory item of information until:

(i) the expiration of the time granted under article seventy-five of the civil practice law and rules for the filing of a petition to vacate or modify an arbitrator's award; (ii) the issue has been a subject of a final judgment; or (iii) where the lessor and the lessee execute a settlement, thirty days after the date a payment is due under the settlement if no payment has been made.

5. (a) Arbitration and enforcement. If a lessor has established or participates in an informal dispute settlement procedure which is consistent in all respects with the provisions of part seven hundred three of title sixteen of the code of federal regulations, any dispute, disparity or con-

flict between any appraisal report prepared by an appraiser licensed by the state department of motor vehicles on behalf of the lessor and one prepared on behalf of the lessee shall be decided by such informal dispute settlement procedure. Lessors utilizing informal dispute settlement procedures pursuant to this subdivision shall insure that the arbitrators participating in such informal dispute settlement procedures are familiar with the provisions of this section.

5. (b) Upon the payment of a prescribed filing fee, a consumer shall have the option of submitting any dispute arising under this section to an alternate arbitration mechanism established pursuant to regulations to be promulgated hereunder by the attorney general. Upon application of the consumer and payment of the filing fee, the lessor shall submit to such alternate arbitration. Such alternate arbitration shall be conducted by a professional arbitrator or arbitration firm appointed by and under regulations established by the attorney general. Such alternate arbitration mechanism shall ensure the personal objectivity of its arbitrators and the right of each party to present its case, to be in attendance during any presentation made by the other party and to rebut or refute such presentation. In all other respects, such alternate arbitration mechanism shall be governed by article seventy-five of the civil practice law and rules. Lessor or lessee shall have thirty days from the date of mailing of a copy of the arbitrator's decision to such lessor or lessee to comply with the terms of such decision.

5. (c) In no event shall any person who has participated in an informal dispute settlement procedure be precluded from seeking the rights or remedies available to such person under applicable law.

5. (d) Nothing in this section shall be deemed to prohibit: (i) the lessor and the lessee from agreeing upon termination of the agreement to the payment by the lessee, in satisfaction of his or her obligation under the provisions of the agreement, of an amount, which the lessor and the lessee agree is a reasonable figure to compensate for damage to the vehicle; (ii) the lessor from retaining any portion of a security deposit in satisfaction of amounts owed to the lessor that are not attributable to excess wear and tear; or (iii) to restrict or otherwise regulate the assessment of charges for excess mileage.

# APPENDIX 4:
# NEW YORK AUTO LEASING ARBITRATION PROGRAM REGULATIONS

## PART 302

### SECTION 302.1 PURPOSE

(a) These regulations are promulgated pursuant to section 343(5)(b) of the Personal Property Law ("PPL") and set forth the procedures for the operation of an alternative arbitration mechanism (the "Program").

(b) These regulations are designed to promote the independent, speedy, efficient and fair disposition of disputes concerning the assessment of excess wear and/or damage to leased vehicles.

### SECTION 302.2 DEFINITIONS

(a) Unless otherwise stated, terms used in these regulations are as defined in PPL Article 9-A.

(b) The term "Administrator" shall mean a professional arbitration firm or individual appointed by the Attorney General to administer the Program.

### SECTION 302.3 APPOINTMENT OF ADMINISTRATOR

(a) The Attorney General shall appoint an Administrator initially to a term not to exceed two years. The term shall be renewable.

(b) The following criteria shall be considered in the selection of an Administrator: capability, objectivity, non-affiliation with a lessor or a lessor's arbitration program, reliability, experience, financial stability, extent of geographic coverage, and fee structure.

(c) The Attorney General shall give appropriate public notice at least 60 days prior to the expiration of an Administrator's term inviting any interested qualified party to apply in writing for the position of Administrator within 30 days from the date of the public notice.

(d) Upon a vacancy occurring prior to the expiration of an Administrator's term, the time periods in subdivision (c) shall not apply and the Attorney General shall take appropriate steps to assure the continued administration of the Program.

## SECTION 302.4 LESSEE'S REQUEST FOR ARBITRATION

(a) The Attorney general shall prescribe and make available a "Request for Arbitration" form. To apply for arbitration under the Program, a lessee shall complete and submit the prescribed form to the Attorney General.

(b) Those lessees wishing a hearing on documents only shall so indicate on the form.

(c) Upon receipt of the submitted form, the Attorney General shall assign a case number and review it for completeness and eligibility and shall accept or reject it.

(e) If the form is rejected, the Attorney General shall promptly return the form to the lessee, indicating in writing the reasons for the rejection and, where possible, inviting the lessee to correct the deficiencies.

(f) If the form is accepted, it shall be referred to the Administrator for processing. The Attorney General shall promptly notify the lessee in writing of the acceptance of the form and of its referral to the Administrator. Upon receipt of the accepted form, the Administrator shall notify the lessee to submit the required filing fee. Upon receipt of the prescribed filing fee, the Administrator shall date stamp the "Request for Arbitration" form. Such date shall be considered the "filing date".

(g) If, after 30 days from the date of the notice of acceptance, the Administrator fails to receive the prescribed filing fee, the Administrator shall promptly advise the lessee in writing that unless such fee is received within 60 days from the date of the notice of acceptance, the form will be returned and the case marked closed. After such time, if the lessee wishes to submit a dispute to the Program, (s)he must submit another "Request for Arbitration" form to the Attorney General.

(h) Participation in any informal dispute resolution mechanism that is not binding on the lessee shall not affect the eligibility of a lessee to participate in the Program.

## SECTION 302.5 ASSIGNMENT OF ARBITRATOR

(a) After the filing date, the Administrator shall assign an arbitrator to hear and decide the case. Notice of assignment shall be mailed to the arbitrator and the parties along with a copy of these regulations and PPL section 343.

(b) The arbitrator assigned shall not have any bias, financial or personal interest in the outcome of the hearing, or current connection to the manufacture, sale, lease, repair or appraisal of motor vehicles.

(c) Upon a finding by the Administrator, at any stage of the process, of grounds to disqualify the arbitrator, the Administrator shall dismiss the arbitrator and assign another arbitrator to the case.

(d) If any arbitrator should resign, die, withdraw or be unable to perform the duties of his/her position, the Administrator shall assign another arbitrator to the case and the period to render a decision shall be extended accordingly.

(e) Arbitrators shall undergo training established by the Administrator and the Attorney General. This training shall include procedural techniques, the duties and responsibilities of arbitrators under the Program, and the substantive provisions of PPL section 343.

## SECTION 302.6 SCHEDULING OF ARBITRATION HEARINGS

(a) The arbitration shall be conducted as an oral hearing unless either party has requested a hearing on documents only and both parties agree to a documents only hearing; provided, however, that the parties may mutually agree in writing to change the mode of hearing. Upon such change, the parties shall notify the Administrator who shall comply with the request and, where necessary, such request shall waive the 40-day limit in which a decision must be rendered.

(b) Within 5 days of the filing date, the Administrator shall send the lessor a copy of the lessee's completed "Request for Arbitration" form together with a notice that it may respond in writing. Such response shall be sent in triplicate, within 15 days of the filing date, to the Administrator, who shall promptly forward a copy to the lessee and to the arbitrator.

(c) The lessee may respond in writing to the lessor's submission within 25 days of the filing date. Such response shall be sent in triplicate to the Administrator, who shall promptly forward a copy to the lessor and to the arbitrator.

(d) An oral hearing, where appropriate, shall be scheduled no later than 35 days from the filing date, unless a later date is agreed to by both parties. The Administrator shall notify both parties of the date, time and place of the hearing at least eight days prior to its scheduled date.

(e) Hearings shall be scheduled to accommodate, where possible, time-of-day needs of the lessee and the lessor, including evening and weekend hours.

(f) Hearings shall also be scheduled to accommodate geographic needs of the lessee and the lessor. Regular hearing sites shall be established at locations designated by the Administrator, including in the following areas: Albany, Binghamton, Buffalo, Nassau County, New York City, Plattsburgh, Poughkeepsie, Rochester, Suffolk County, Syracuse, Utica, Watertown and Westchester. No hearing site established by the Administrator shall be discontinued without the approval of the Attorney General. In addition, where a regular site is more than 100 miles from the lessee's residence, a hearing must be scheduled at the request of the lessee at a location designated by the Administrator within 100 miles of the lessee's residence.

(g) A party may present its case by telephone, provided that adequate advance notice is given to the Administrator and the consent of the other party is obtained. In such cases, the arbitrator and both parties shall be included and the party requesting the telephonic hearing shall pay all costs associated therewith.

## SECTION 302.7 ADJOURNMENTS

Either party may make a request to reschedule the hearing. Except in unusual circumstances, such request shall be made to the Administrator orally or in writing at least two business days prior to the hearing date. Upon a finding of good cause, the arbitrator may reschedule the hearing. In unusual circumstances, the arbitrator may reschedule the hearing at any time prior to its commencement.

## SECTION 302.8 REQUEST FOR ADDITIONAL INFORMATION OR DOCUMENTS

(a) A party, by application in writing to the Administrator, may request the arbitrator to direct the other party to produce any documents or information. The arbitrator shall, upon receiving such request, or on his or her own initiative, direct the production of documents or information which she or he believes will reasonably assist a party in presenting his or her case or assist the arbitrator in deciding the case. The arbitrator's direction for the production of documents and information shall allow a reasonable time for the gathering and production of such documents and information.

(b) All documents and information forwarded in compliance with the arbitrator's direction shall be legible and received no later than three business days prior to the date of the hearing. Each party shall bear its own photocopying costs.

(c) Upon failure of a party to comply with the arbitrator's direction to produce documents and/or information, the arbitrator may draw a negative inference concerning any issue involving such documents or information.

(d) The term "documents" in this section shall include, but not be limited to, relevant manufacturer's service bulletins, dealer work orders, diagnoses, repair bills, damage appraisals and all communications relating to the issue of excessive wear or damage.

(e) At the request of either party or on his or her own initiative, the arbitrator may subpoena any witnesses to appear or documents to be presented at the hearing.

## SECTION 302.9 REPRESENTATION BY COUNSEL OR THIRD PARTY

Any party may be represented by counsel or assisted by any third party.

## SECTION 302.10 INTERPRETERS

Any party wishing an interpreter shall make the necessary arrangements and assume the costs for such service.

## SECTION 302.11 HEARING PROCEDURE

(a) The conduct of the hearing shall afford each party a full and equal opportunity to present his/her case.

(b) The arbitrator shall administer an oath or affirmation to each individual who testifies.

(c) Formal rules of evidence shall not apply; the parties may introduce any evidence which the arbitrator agrees is relevant.

(d) The arbitrator shall receive in evidence a decision rendered in a previous arbitration which was not binding on the lessee and give it such weight as the arbitrator deems appropriate.

(e) The arbitrator shall receive relevant evidence of witnesses by affidavit, and such affidavits shall be given such weight as the arbitrator deems appropriate.

(f) The arbitrator shall have discretion to examine or ride in the lessee's vehicle, if available. Both parties shall be afforded the opportunity to be present and accompany the arbitrator on any such examination or ride.

(g) The lessee shall first present his/her evidence and the lessor shall then present its evidence. Each party may question the witnesses called by the other. The arbitrator may question any party or witness at any time during the hearing.

(h) A party has the right to make a record of the hearing. The arbitrator shall maintain decorum at the hearing.

(i) The arbitrator may request additional evidence after the closing the hearing. All such evidence shall be submitted to the Administrator for transmission to the arbitrator and the parties.

## SECTION 302.12 HEARING ON DOCUMENTS ONLY

If the hearing is on documents only, all documents shall be submitted to the Administrator no later than 30 days from the filing date. The arbitrator shall render a timely decision based on all documents submitted.

## SECTION 302.13 DEFAULTS

(a) Upon the failure of a party to appear at an oral hearing, the arbitrator shall nevertheless conduct the hearing and render a timely decision based on the evidence presented and documents contained in the file.

(b) If neither party appears at the hearing, the arbitrator shall return the case to the Administrator who shall close it and so notify the parties.

(c) In a documents-only hearing, where the lessor fails to respond, the arbitrator shall render a decision based upon the documents contained in the file.

## SECTION 302.14 WITHDRAWAL OR SETTLEMENT PRIOR TO DECISION

(a) A lessee may withdraw his/her request for arbitration at any time prior to decision. If the Administrator is notified by the lessee of his/her request to withdraw within seven business days of the filing date, the Administrator shall refund the filing fee.

(b) If the parties agree to a settlement more than seven business days after the filing date but prior to the issuance of a decision, they shall notify the Administrator in writing of the terms of the settlement. Upon the request of the parties, the arbitrator shall issue a decision reflecting the settlement.

## SECTION 302.15 THE DECISION

(a) The arbitrator shall render a decision within 40 days of the filing date which shall be in writing on a form prescribed by the Attorney General. The decision shall be dated and signed by the arbitrator.

(b) The decision shall indicate whether there was any excess wear and/or damage to the vehicle for which the lessee is responsible and, where applicable, specify the amount of such excess wear and/or damage. A basis for the arbitrator's findings and calculations shall be included in the decision. The decision shall also award the prescribed filing fee to a successful lessee.

(c) The decision shall, where applicable, require that any action or payment be completed within 30 days from the date the Administrator notifies the lessor in writing of the decision, unless the parties agree to an extended time.

(d) The Administrator shall review the decision for technical completeness and accuracy and advise the arbitrator of any suggested technical corrections, such as computational, typographical or other minor corrections. Such changes shall be made only with the consent of the arbitrator.

(e) After review, the Administrator shall, within 45 days of the filing date, mail a copy of the final decision to both parties, the arbitrator, and the Attorney General. The date of mailing to the parties shall be date-stamped by the Administrator on the decision as the date of issuance.

(f) Failure to mail the decision to the parties within the specified time period or failure to hold the hearing within the prescribed time shall not invalidate the decision.

(g) The arbitrator's decision is binding on both parties and is final, subject only to judicial review pursuant to CPLR, Article 75. The decision shall include a statement to this effect.

## SECTION 302.16 RECORD KEEPING

The Administrator shall keep all records pertaining to each arbitration for a period of at least two years and shall make the records of a particular arbitration available for inspection upon written request by a party to that arbitration, and shall make records of all arbitrations available to the Attorney General upon written request.

## SECTION 302.17 MISCELLANEOUS PROVISIONS

(a) All communications between the parties and the arbitrator, other than at oral hearings, shall be directed to the Administrator.

(b) If any provision of these regulations or the application of such provision to any persons or circumstances shall be held invalid, the validity of the remainder of these regulations and the applicability of such provision to other persons or circumstances shall not be affected thereby.

# APPENDIX 5:
# CONSUMER LEASING—REGULATION M
# [12 CFR 213]

### § 213.1 AUTHORITY, SCOPE, PURPOSE, AND ENFORCEMENT.

(a) Authority. The regulation in this part, known as Regulation M, is issued by the Board of Governors of the Federal Reserve System to implement the consumer leasing provisions of the Truth in Lending Act, which is Title I of the Consumer Credit Protection Act, as amended (15 U.S.C. 1601 et seq.). Information collection requirements contained in this regulation have been approved by the Office of Management and Budget under the provisions of 44 U.S.C. 3501 et seq. and have been assigned OMB control number 7100–0202.

(b) Scope and purpose. This part applies to all persons that are lessors of personal property under consumer leases as those terms are defined in §213.2(e)(1) and (h). The purpose of this part is:

(1) To ensure that lessees of personal property receive meaningful disclosures that enable them to compare lease terms with other leases and, where appropriate, with credit transactions;

(2) To limit the amount of balloon payments in consumer lease transactions; and

(3) To provide for the accurate disclosure of lease terms in advertising.

(c) Enforcement and liability. Section 108 of the act contains the administrative enforcement provisions. Sections 112, 130, 131, and 185 of the act contain the liability provisions for failing to comply with the requirements of the act and this part.

## § 213.2 DEFINITIONS.

For the purposes of this part the following definitions apply:

(a) Act means the Truth in Lending Act (15 U.S.C. 1601 et seq.) and the Consumer Leasing Act is chapter 5 of the Truth in Lending Act.

(b) Advertisement means a commercial message in any medium that directly or indirectly promotes a consumer lease transaction.

(c) Board refers to the Board of Governors of the Federal Reserve System.

(d) Closed-end lease means a consumer lease other than an open-end lease as defined in this section.

(e)(1) Consumer lease means a contract in the form of a bailment or lease for the use of personal property by a natural person primarily for personal, family, or household purposes, for a period exceeding four months and for a total contractual obligation not exceeding $25,000, whether or not the lessee has the option to purchase or otherwise become the owner of the property at the expiration of the lease. Unless the context indicates otherwise, in this part "lease" means "consumer lease."

> (2) The term does not include a lease that meets the definition of a credit sale in Regulation Z (12 CFR 226.2(a)). It also does not include a lease for agricultural, business, or commercial purposes or a lease made to an organization.

> (3) This part does not apply to a lease transaction of personal property which is incident to the lease of real property and which provides that:

> > (i) The lessee has no liability for the value of the personal property at the end of the lease term except for abnormal wear and tear; and

> > (ii) The lessee has no option to purchase the leased property.

(f) Gross capitalized cost means the amount agreed upon by the lessor and the lessee as the value of the leased property and any items that are capitalized or amortized during the lease term, including but not limited to taxes, insurance, service agreements, and any outstanding prior credit or lease balance. Capitalized cost reduction means the total amount of any rebate, cash payment, net trade-in allowance, and non-cash credit that reduces the gross capitalized cost. The adjusted capitalized cost equals the gross capitalized cost less the capitalized cost reduction, and is the amount used by the lessor in calculating the base periodic payment.

(g) Lessee means a natural person who enters into or is offered a consumer lease.

(h) Lessor means a person who regularly leases, offers to lease, or arranges for the lease of personal property under a consumer lease. A person who has leased, offered, or arranged to lease personal property more than five times in the preceding calendar year or more than five times in the current calendar year is subject to the act and this part.

(i) Open-end lease means a consumer lease in which the lessee's liability at the end of the lease term is based on the difference between the residual value of the leased property and its realized value.

(j) Organization means a corporation, trust, estate, partnership, cooperative, association, or government entity or instrumentality.

(k) Person means a natural person or an organization.

(l) Personal property means any property that is not real property under the law of the state where the property is located at the time it is offered or made available for lease.

(m) Realized value means:

(1) The price received by the lessor for the leased property at disposition;

(2) The highest offer for disposition of the leased property; or

(3) The fair market value of the leased property at the end of the lease term.

(n) Residual value means the value of the leased property at the end of the lease term, as estimated or assigned at consummation by the lessor, used in calculating the base periodic payment.

(o) Security interest and security mean any interest in property that secures the payment or performance of an obligation.

(p) State means any state, the District of Columbia, the Commonwealth of Puerto Rico, and any territory or possession of the United States.

## § 213.3 GENERAL DISCLOSURE REQUIREMENTS.

(a) General requirements. A lessor shall make the disclosures required by §213.4, as applicable. The disclosures shall be made clearly and conspicuously in writing in a form the consumer may keep, in accordance with this section.

(1) Form of disclosures. The disclosures required by §213.4 shall be given to the lessee together in a dated statement that identifies the lessor and the lessee; the disclosures may be made either in a separate statement that identifies the consumer lease transaction or in the contract or other document evidencing the lease. Alternatively, the disclosures required to be segregated from other information un-

der paragraph (a)(2) of this section may be provided in a separate dated statement that identifies the lease, and the other required disclosures may be provided in the lease contract or other document evidencing the lease. In a lease of multiple items, the property description required by §213.4(a) may be given in a separate statement that is incorporated by reference in the disclosure statement required by this paragraph.

(2) Segregation of certain disclosures. The following disclosures shall be segregated from other information and shall contain only directly related information: §§213.4(b) through (f), (g)(2), (h)(3), (i)(1), (j), and (m)(1). The headings, content, and format for the disclosures referred to in this paragraph (a)(2) shall be provided in a manner substantially similar to the applicable model form in appendix A of this part.

(3) Timing of disclosures. A lessor shall provide the disclosures to the lessee prior to the consummation of a consumer lease.

(4) Language of disclosures. The disclosures required by §213.4 may be made in a language other than English provided that they are made available in English upon the lessee's request.

(5) Electronic communication. For rules governing the electronic delivery of disclosures, including a definition of electronic communication, see §213.6.

(b) Additional information; nonsegregated disclosures. Additional information may be provided with any disclosure not listed in paragraph (a)(2) of this section, but it shall not be stated, used, or placed so as to mislead or confuse the lessee or contradict, obscure, or detract attention from any disclosure required by this part.

(c) Multiple lessors or lessees. When a transaction involves more than one lessor, the disclosures required by this part may be made by one lessor on behalf of all the lessors. When a lease involves more than one lessee, the lessor may provide the disclosures to any lessee who is primarily liable on the lease.

(d) Use of estimates. If an amount or other item needed to comply with a required disclosure is unknown or unavailable after reasonable efforts have been made to ascertain the information, the lessor may use a reasonable estimate that is based on the best information available to the lessor, is clearly identified as an estimate, and is not used to circumvent or evade any disclosures required by this part.

(e) Effect of subsequent occurrence. If a required disclosure becomes inaccurate because of an event occurring after consummation, the inaccuracy is not a violation of this part.

(f) Minor variations. A lessor may disregard the effects of the following in making disclosures:

(1) That payments must be collected in whole cents;

(2) That dates of scheduled payments may be different because a scheduled date is not a business day;

(3) That months have different numbers of days; and

(4) That February 29 occurs in a leap year.

## § 213.4 CONTENT OF DISCLOSURES.

For any consumer lease subject to this part, the lessor shall disclose the following information, as applicable:

(a) Description of property. A brief description of the leased property sufficient to identify the property to the lessee and lessor.

(b) Amount due at lease signing or delivery. The total amount to be paid prior to or at consummation or by delivery, if delivery occurs after consummation, using the term "amount due at lease signing or delivery." The lessor shall itemize each component by type and amount, including any refundable security deposit, advance monthly or other periodic payment, and capitalized cost reduction; and in motor-vehicle leases, shall itemize how the amount due will be paid, by type and amount, including any net trade-in allowance, rebates, noncash credits, and cash payments in a format substantially similar to the model forms in appendix A of this part.

(c) Payment schedule and total amount of periodic payments. The number, amount, and due dates or periods of payments scheduled under the lease, and the total amount of the periodic payments.

(d) Other charges. The total amount of other charges payable to the lessor, itemized by type and amount, that are not included in the periodic payments. Such charges include the amount of any liability the lease imposes upon the lessee at the end of the lease term; the potential difference between the residual and realized values referred to in paragraph (k) of this section is excluded.

(e) Total of payments. The total of payments, with a description such as "the amount you will have paid by the end of the lease." This amount is the sum of the amount due at lease signing (less any refundable amounts), the total amount of periodic payments (less any portion of the periodic payment paid at lease signing), and other charges under paragraphs (b), (c), and (d) of this section. In an open-end lease, a description such as "you will owe an additional amount if the actual value of the vehicle is less than the residual value" shall accompany the disclosure.

(f) Payment calculation. In a motor-vehicle lease, a mathematical progression of how the scheduled periodic payment is derived, in a format substantially similar to the applicable model form in appendix A of this part, which shall contain the following:

(1) Gross capitalized cost. The gross capitalized cost, including a disclosure of the agreed upon value of the vehicle, a description such as "the agreed upon value of the vehicle [state the amount] and any items you pay for over the lease term (such as service contracts, insurance, and any outstanding prior credit or lease balance)," and a statement of the lessee's option to receive a separate written itemization of the gross capitalized cost. If requested by the lessee, the itemization shall be provided before consummation.

(2) Capitalized cost reduction. The capitalized cost reduction, with a description such as "the amount of any net trade-in allowance, rebate, noncash credit, or cash you pay that reduces the gross capitalized cost."

(3) Adjusted capitalized cost. The adjusted capitalized cost, with a description such as "the amount used in calculating your base [periodic] payment."

(4) Residual value. The residual value, with a description such as "the value of the vehicle at the end of the lease used in calculating your base [periodic] payment."

(5) Depreciation and any amortized amounts. The depreciation and any amortized amounts, which is the difference between the adjusted capitalized cost and the residual value, with a description such as "the amount charged for the vehicle's decline in value through normal use and for any other items paid over the lease term."

(6) Rent charge. The rent charge, with a description such as "the amount charged in addition to the depreciation and any amortized amounts." This amount is the difference between the total of the base periodic payments over the lease term minus the depreciation and any amortized amounts.

(7) Total of base periodic payments. The total of base periodic payments with a description such as "depreciation and any amortized amounts plus the rent charge."

(8) Lease payments. The lease payments with a description such as "the number of payments in your lease."

(9) Base periodic payment. The total of the base periodic payments divided by the number of payment periods in the lease.

(10) Itemization of other charges. An itemization of any other charges that are part of the periodic payment.

(11) Total periodic payment. The sum of the base periodic payment and any other charges that are part of the periodic payment.

(g) Early termination—(1) Conditions and disclosure of charges. A statement of the conditions under which the lessee or lessor may terminate the lease prior to the end of the lease term; and the amount or a description of the method for determining the amount of any penalty or other charge for early termination, which must be reasonable.

(2) Early-termination notice. In a motor-vehicle lease, a notice substantially similar to the following: "Early Termination. You may have to pay a substantial charge if you end this lease early. The charge may be up to several thousand dollars. The actual charge will depend on when the lease is terminated. The earlier you end the lease, the greater this charge is likely to be."

(h) Maintenance responsibilities. The following provisions are required:

(1) Statement of responsibilities. A statement specifying whether the lessor or the lessee is responsible for maintaining or servicing the leased property, together with a brief description of the responsibility;

(2) Wear and use standard. A statement of the lessor's standards for wear and use (if any), which must be reasonable; and

(3) Notice of wear and use standard. In a motor-vehicle lease, a notice regarding wear and use substantially similar to the following: "Excessive Wear and Use. You may be charged for excessive wear based on our standards for normal use." The notice shall also specify the amount or method for determining any charge for excess mileage.

(i) Purchase option. A statement of whether or not the lessee has the option to purchase the leased property, and:

(1) End of lease term. If at the end of the lease term, the purchase price; and

(2) During lease term. If prior to the end of the lease term, the purchase price or the method for determining the price and when the lessee may exercise this option.

(j) Statement referencing nonsegregated disclosures. A statement that the lessee should refer to the lease documents for additional information on early termination, purchase options and maintenance responsibilities, warranties, late and default charges, insurance, and any security interests, if applicable.

(k) Liability between residual and realized values. A statement of the lessee's liability, if any, at early termination or at the end of the lease term for the difference between the residual value of the leased property and its realized value.

(l) Right of appraisal. If the lessee's liability at early termination or at the end of the lease term is based on the realized value of the leased property, a statement that the lessee may obtain, at the lessee's expense, a professional appraisal by an independent third party (agreed to by the lessee and the lessor) of the value that could be realized at sale of the leased property. The appraisal shall be final and binding on the parties.

(m) Liability at end of lease term based on residual value. If the lessee is liable at the end of the lease term for the difference between the residual value of the leased property and its realized value:

(1) Rent and other charges. The rent and other charges, paid by the lessee and required by the lessor as an incident to the lease transaction, with a description such as "the total amount of rent and other charges imposed in connection with your lease [state the amount]."

(2) Excess liability. A statement about a rebuttable presumption that, at the end of the lease term, the residual value of the leased property is unreasonable and not in good faith to the extent that the residual value exceeds the realized value by more than three times the base monthly payment (or more than three times the average payment allocable to a monthly period, if the lease calls for periodic payments other than monthly); and that the lessor cannot collect the excess amount unless the lessor brings a successful court action and pays the lessee's reasonable attorney's fees, or unless the excess of the residual value over the realized value is due to unreasonable or excessive wear or use of the leased property (in which case the rebuttable presumption does not apply).

(3) Mutually agreeable final adjustment. A statement that the lessee and lessor are permitted, after termination of the lease, to make any mutually agreeable final adjustment regarding excess liability.

(n) Fees and taxes. The total dollar amount for all official and license fees, registration, title, or taxes required to be paid in connection with the lease.

(o) Insurance. A brief identification of insurance in connection with the lease including:

(1) Through the lessor. If the insurance is provided by or paid through the lessor, the types and amounts of coverage and the cost to the lessee; or

(2) Through a third party. If the lessee must obtain the insurance, the types and amounts of coverage required of the lessee.

(p) Warranties or guarantees. A statement identifying all express warranties and guarantees from the manufacturer or lessor with respect to the leased property that apply to the lessee.

(q) Penalties and other charges for delinquency. The amount or the method of determining the amount of any penalty or other charge for delinquency, default, or late payments, which must be reasonable.

(r) Security interest. A description of any security interest, other than a security deposit disclosed under paragraph (b) of this section, held or to be retained by the lessor; and a clear identification of the property to which the security interest relates.

(s) Limitations on rate information. If a lessor provides a percentage rate in an advertisement or in documents evidencing the lease transaction, a notice stating that "this percentage may not measure the overall cost of financing this lease" shall accompany the rate disclosure. The lessor shall not use the term "annual percentage rate," "annual lease rate," or any equivalent term.

(t) Non-motor vehicle open-end leases. Non-motor vehicle open-end leases remain subject to section 182(10) of the act regarding end of term liability.

## § 213.5 RENEGOTIATIONS, EXTENSIONS, AND ASSUMPTIONS.

(a) Renegotiation. A renegotiation occurs when a consumer lease subject to this part is satisfied and replaced by a new lease undertaken by the same consumer. A renegotiation requires new disclosures, except as provided in paragraph (d) of this section.

(b) Extension. An extension is a continuation, agreed to by the lessor and the lessee, of an existing consumer lease beyond the originally scheduled end of the lease term, except when the continuation is the result of a renegotiation. An extension that exceeds six months requires new disclosures, except as provided in paragraph (d) of this section.

(c) Assumption. New disclosures are not required when a consumer lease is assumed by another person, whether or not the lessor charges an assumption fee.

(d) Exceptions. New disclosures are not required for the following, even if they meet the definition of a renegotiation or an extension:

(1) A reduction in the rent charge;

(2) The deferment of one or more payments, whether or not a fee is charged;

(3) The extension of a lease for not more than six months on a month-to-month basis or otherwise;

(4) A substitution of leased property with property that has a substantially equivalent or greater economic value, provided no other lease terms are changed;

(5) The addition, deletion, or substitution of leased property in a multiple-item lease, provided the average periodic payment does not change by more than 25 percent; or

(6) An agreement resulting from a court proceeding.

## § 213.6 ELECTRONIC COMMUNICATION.

(a) Definition. "Electronic communication" means a message transmitted electronically between a lessor and a lessee in a format that allows visual text to be displayed on equipment, for example, a personal computer monitor.

(b) General rule. In accordance with the Electronic Signatures in Global and National Commerce Act (the E-Sign Act) (15 U.S.C. 7001 et seq.) and the rules of this part, a lessor may provide by electronic communication any disclosure required by this part to be in writing.

(c) When consent is required. Under the E-Sign Act, a lessor is required to obtain a lessee's affirmative consent when providing disclosures related to a transaction. For purposes of this requirement, the disclosures required under §213.7 are deemed not to be related to a transaction.

(d) Address or location to receive electronic communication. A lessor that uses electronic communication to provide disclosures required by this part shall:

(1) Send the disclosure to the consumer's electronic address; or

(2) Make the disclosure available at another location such as a web site; and

(i) Alert the lessee of the disclosure's availability by sending a notice to the consumer's electronic address (or to a postal address, at the lessor's option). The notice shall identify the transaction involved and the address of the Internet web site or other location where the disclosure is available; and

(ii) Make the disclosure available for at least 90 days from the date the disclosure first becomes available or from the date of the notice alerting the lessee of the disclosure, whichever comes later.

(3) Exceptions. A lessor need not comply with paragraph (d)(2)(i) and (ii) of this section for the disclosures required under §213.7.

(e) Redelivery. When a disclosure provided by electronic communication is returned to a lessor undelivered, the lessor shall take reasonable steps to attempt redelivery using information in its files.

### § 213.7 ADVERTISING.

(a) General rule. An advertisement for a consumer lease may state that a specific lease of property at specific amounts or terms is available only if the lessor usually and customarily leases or will lease the property at those amounts or terms.

(b) Clear and conspicuous standard. Disclosures required by this section shall be made clearly and conspicuously.

(1) Amount due at lease signing or delivery. Except for the statement of a periodic payment, any affirmative or negative reference to a charge that is a part of the disclosure required under paragraph (d)(2)(ii) of this section shall not be more prominent than that disclosure.

(2) Advertisement of a lease rate. If a lessor provides a percentage rate in an advertisement, the rate shall not be more prominent than any of the disclosures in §213.4, with the exception of the notice in §213.4(s) required to accompany the rate; and the lessor shall not use the term "annual percentage rate," "annual lease rate," or equivalent term.

(c) Catalogs and multipage advertisements. A catalog or other multipage advertisement that provides a table or schedule of the required disclosures shall be considered a single advertisement if, for lease terms that appear without all the required disclosures, the advertisement refers to the page or pages on which the table or schedule appears.

(d) Advertisement of terms that require additional disclosure—(1) Triggering terms. An advertisement that states any of the following items shall contain the disclosures required by paragraph (d)(2) of this section, except as provided in paragraphs (e) and (f) of this section:

(i) The amount of any payment; or

(ii) A statement of any capitalized cost reduction or other payment (or that no payment is required) prior to or at consummation or by delivery, if delivery occurs after consummation.

(2) Additional terms. An advertisement stating any item listed in paragraph (d)(1) of this section shall also state the following items:

(i) That the transaction advertised is a lease;

(ii) The total amount due prior to or at consummation or by delivery, if delivery occurs after consummation;

(iii) The number, amounts, and due dates or periods of scheduled payments under the lease;

(iv) A statement of whether or not a security deposit is required; and

(v) A statement that an extra charge may be imposed at the end of the lease term where the lessee's liability (if any) is based on the difference between the residual value of the leased property and its realized value at the end of the lease term.

(e) Alternative disclosures—merchandise tags. A merchandise tag stating any item listed in paragraph (d)(1) of this section may comply with paragraph (d)(2) of this section by referring to a sign or display prominently posted in the lessor's place of business that contains a table or schedule of the required disclosures.

(f) Alternative disclosures—television or radio advertisements.—(1) Toll-free number or print advertisement. An advertisement made through television or radio stating any item listed in paragraph (d)(1) of this section complies with paragraph (d)(2) of this section if the advertisement states the items listed in paragraphs (d)(2)(i) through (iii) of this section, and:

(i) Lists a toll-free telephone number along with a reference that such number may be used by consumers to obtain the information required by paragraph (d)(2) of this section; or

(ii) Directs the consumer to a written advertisement in a publication of general circulation in the community served by the media station, including the name and the date of the publication, with a statement that information required by paragraph (d)(2) of this section is included in the advertisement. The written advertisement shall be published beginning at least three days before and ending at least ten days after the broadcast.

(2) Establishment of toll-free number. (i) The toll-free telephone number shall be available for no fewer than ten days, beginning on the date of the broadcast.

(ii) The lessor shall provide the information required by paragraph (d)(2) of this section orally, or in writing upon request.

## § 213.8 RECORD RETENTION.

A lessor shall retain evidence of compliance with the requirements imposed by this part, other than the advertising requirements under §213.7, for a period of not less than two years after the date the disclosures are required to be made or an action is required to be taken.

## § 213.9 RELATION TO STATE LAWS.

(a) Inconsistent state law. A state law that is inconsistent with the requirements of the act and this part is preempted to the extent of the inconsistency. If a lessor cannot comply with a state law without violating a provision of this part, the state law is inconsistent within the meaning of section 186(a) of the act and is preempted, unless the state law gives greater protection and benefit to the consumer. A state, through an official having primary enforcement or interpretative responsibilities for the state consumer leasing law, may apply to the Board for a preemption determination.

(b) Exemptions.—(1) Application. A state may apply to the Board for an exemption from the requirements of the act and this part for any class of lease transactions within the state. The Board will grant such an exemption if the Board determines that:

(i) The class of leasing transactions is subject to state law requirements substantially similar to the act and this part or that lessees are afforded greater protection under state law; and

(ii) There is adequate provision for state enforcement.

(2) Enforcement and liability. After an exemption has been granted, the requirements of the applicable state law (except for additional requirements not imposed by federal law) will constitute the requirements of the act and this part. No exemption will extend to the civil liability provisions of sections 130, 131, and 185 of the act.

# APPENDIX 6:
# MODEL FEDERAL CONSUMER LEASING ACT DISCLOSURES FORM

Appendix A-2 Model Closed-End or Net Vehicle Lease Disclosures

## Federal Consumer Leasing Act Disclosures

Date _____

Lessor(s) _____     Lessee(s) _____

| Amount Due at Lease Signing or Delivery (Itemized below)* | Monthly Payments | Other Charges (not part of your monthly payment) | Total of Payments (The amount you will have paid by the end of the lease) |
|---|---|---|---|
| $ _____ | Your first monthly payment of $ _____ is due on _____, followed by _____ payments of $ _____ due on the _____ of each month. The total of your monthly payments is $ _____. | Disposition fee (if you do not purchase the vehicle)  $ _____   Total  $ _____ | $ _____ |

### * Itemization of Amount Due at Lease Signing or Delivery

Amount Due at Lease Signing or Delivery:      How the Amount Due at Lease Signing or Delivery will be paid:

| | | | |
|---|---|---|---|
| Capitalized cost reduction | $ _____ | Net trade-in allowance | $ _____ |
| First monthly payment | _____ | Rebates and noncash credits | _____ |
| Refundable security deposit | _____ | Amount to be paid in cash | _____ |
| Title fees | _____ | | |
| Registration fees | _____ | | |
| _____ | | | |
| Total | $ _____ | Total | $ _____ |

### Your monthly payment is determined as shown below:

Gross capitalized cost. The agreed upon value of the vehicle ($ _____ ) and any items you pay over the lease term (such as service contracts, insurance, and any outstanding prior credit or lease balance) ....................................................................................................  $ _____

If you want an itemization of this amount, please check this box. ☐

Capitalized cost reduction. The amount of any net trade-in allowance, rebate, noncash credit, or cash you pay that reduces the gross capitalized cost ....................................................................  − _____

Adjusted capitalized cost. The amount used in calculating your base monthly payment .......................  = _____

Residual value. The value of the vehicle at the end of the lease used in calculating your base monthly payment ..........  − _____

Depreciation and any amortized amounts. The amount charged for the vehicle's decline in value through normal use and for other items paid over the lease term ....................................................  = _____

Rent charge. The amount charged in addition to the depreciation and any amortized amounts .....................  + _____

Total of base monthly payments. The depreciation and any amortized amounts plus the rent charge .......................  = _____

Lease payments. The number of payments in your lease ..........................................................  ÷ _____

Base monthly payment ...................................................................................................  = _____

Monthly sales/use tax ...................................................................................................  + _____

_____ ...................................................................................................  = $ _____

Total monthly payment ...................................................................................................

---

**Early Termination.** You may have to pay a substantial charge if you end this lease early. The charge may be up to several thousand dollars. The actual charge will depend on when the lease is terminated. The earlier you end the lease, the greater this charge is likely to be.

**Excessive Wear and Use.** You may be charged for excessive wear based on our standards for normal use [and for mileage in excess of _____ miles per year at the rate of _____ per mile].

**Purchase Option at End of Lease Term.** [You have an option to purchase the vehicle at the end of the lease term for $ _____ [and a purchase option fee of $ _____ ].] [You do not have an option to purchase the vehicle at the end of the lease term.]

**Other Important Terms.** See your lease documents for additional information on early termination, purchase options and maintenance responsibilities, warranties, late and default charges, insurance, and any security interest, if applicable.

# MODEL FEDERAL CONSUMER LEASING ACT DISCLOSURES FORM

Appendix A-2 Model Closed-End or Net Vehicle Lease Disclosures

## Federal Consumer Leasing Act Disclosures

Date _____

Lessor(s) _____    Lessee(s) _____

| Amount Due at Lease Signing or Delivery (Itemized below)* | Monthly Payments | Other Charges (not part of your monthly payment) | Total of Payments (The amount you will have paid by the end of the lease) |
|---|---|---|---|
| $ _____ | Your first monthly payment of $ _____ is due on _____, followed by _____ payments of $ _____ due on the _____ of each month. The total of your monthly payments is $ _____. | Disposition fee (if you do not purchase the vehicle) $ _____ _____ _____  Total  $ _____ | $ _____ |

### * Itemization of Amount Due at Lease Signing or Delivery

| Amount Due at Lease Signing or Delivery: | | How the Amount Due at Lease Signing or Delivery will be paid: | |
|---|---|---|---|
| Capitalized cost reduction | $ _____ | Net trade-in allowance | $ _____ |
| First monthly payment | _____ | Rebates and noncash credits | _____ |
| Refundable security deposit | _____ | Amount to be paid in cash | _____ |
| Title fees | _____ | _____ | _____ |
| Registration fees | _____ | | |
| _____ | | | |
| Total | $ _____ | Total | $ _____ |

### Your monthly payment is determined as shown below:

**Gross capitalized cost.** The agreed upon value of the vehicle ($ _____ ) and any items you pay over the lease term (such as service contracts, insurance, and any outstanding prior credit or lease balance) ................................................................ $ _____

If you want an itemization of this amount, please check this box. ☐

**Capitalized cost reduction.** The amount of any net trade-in allowance, rebate, noncash credit, or cash you pay that reduces the gross capitalized cost ................................................ − _____

**Adjusted capitalized cost.** The amount used in calculating your base monthly payment ................................ = _____

**Residual value.** The value of the vehicle at the end of the lease used in calculating your base monthly payment ............ − _____

**Depreciation and any amortized amounts.** The amount charged for the vehicle's decline in value through normal use and for other items paid over the lease term ................................ = _____

**Rent charge.** The amount charged in addition to the depreciation and any amortized amounts ................................ + _____

**Total of base monthly payments.** The depreciation and any amortized amounts plus the rent charge ................ = _____

**Lease payments.** The number of payments in your lease ................................ ÷ _____

**Base monthly payment** ................................................................ = _____

**Monthly sales/use tax** ................................................................ + _____

_____ ................................................................ + _____

**Total monthly payment** ................................................................ = $ _____

> **Early Termination. You may have to pay a substantial charge if you end this lease early. The charge may be up to several thousand dollars. The actual charge will depend on when the lease is terminated. The earlier you end the lease, the greater this charge is likely to be.**

**Excessive Wear and Use.** You may be charged for excessive wear based on our standards for normal use [and for mileage in excess of _____ miles per year at the rate of _____ per mile].

**Purchase Option at End of Lease Term.** [You have an option to purchase the vehicle at the end of the lease term for $ _____ [and a purchase option fee of $ _____ ].] [You do not have an option to purchase the vehicle at the end of the lease term.]

**Other Important Terms.** See your lease documents for additional information on early termination, purchase options and maintenance responsibilities, warranties, late and default charges, insurance, and any security interest, if applicable.

# GLOSSARY

**Acquisition Fee**—Also known as an administrative fee, assignment fee or bank fee, refers to a charge included in most lease transactions to cover administrative or insurance costs, such as the cost of obtaining a credit report, verifying insurance coverage, checking the accuracy and completeness of the lease documentation, entering the lease in data processing and accounting systems, and purchasing insurance for or reserving funds for residual-value losses, gap-coverage losses, and other lease losses. The fee is usually paid up front or included in the gross capitalized cost.

**Additional Insured**—A party that is covered by another party's insurance policy, e.g., the lessor or assignee.

**Adjusted Capitalized Cost**—Also known as an adjusted cap cost or net cap cost, refers to the amount capitalized at the beginning of the lease, equal to the gross capitalized cost minus the capitalized cost reduction.

**Amortized Amounts**—Amounts, which may include taxes, fees, charges for service contracts, payments for insurance, and any prior credit or lease balance, that are included in the gross capitalized cost and are paid as part of the base monthly payment.

**Amount Due at Lease Signing or Delivery**—The total of any capitalized cost reduction, monthly payments paid at signing, security deposit, title and registration fees, and other amounts due before the lessee takes delivery of the vehicle.

**Annual Percentage Rate (APR)**—The annualized cost of credit expressed as a percentage. The APR is used in finance agreements not leasing agreements.

**Assignee**—A third party that buys a lease agreement from a lessor, at which point the person leasing the car becomes obligated to the assignee, and the assignee generally assumes the responsibilities of the lessor.

**Assignment**—The sale of a lease agreement and transfer of the ownership rights for the leased vehicle from the lessor to an assignee. Many leases are assigned at the time the lease is signed.

**Assignor**—A lessor that sells the lease agreement and transfers the ownership rights for the leased vehicle to an assignee.

**Base Monthly Payment**—The portion of the monthly payment that covers depreciation, any amortized amounts, and rent charges, that is calculated by adding the amount of depreciation, any other amortized amounts, and rent charges and dividing the total by the number of months in the lease. Monthly sales/use taxes and other monthly fees are added to this base monthly payment to determine the total monthly payment.

**Broker**—Also known as an arranger, refers to an entity that arranges for the sale or lease of vehicles through another party.

**Business Lease**—A lease of personal property to (1) an individual to be used primarily for business, commercial, or agricultural purposes; or (2) an organization, such as a partnership, corporation, or government agency.

**Capitalized Cost**—Shortened term for either gross capitalized cost or adjusted capitalized cost.

**Capitalized Cost Reduction**—Also known as a cap cost reduction, refers to the sum of any down payment, net trade-in allowance, and rebate used to reduce the gross capitalized cost.

**Captive Finance Company**—A finance company related to a particular automobile manufacturer or distributor.

**Closed-End Lease**—Also known as a walk-away lease, refers to a lease in which the lessee is not responsible for the difference if the actual value of the vehicle at the scheduled end of the lease is less than the residual.

**Consumer Lease**—A lease of personal property to an individual to be used primarily for personal, family, or household purposes for a period of more than 4 months and with a total contractual obligation of no more than $25,000.

**Consumer Leasing Act**—A 1976 amendment to the federal Truth in Lending Act that requires disclosure of the cost and terms of consumer leases and also places substantive restrictions on consumer leases.

**Constant Yield Method**—Also known as the actuarial method, refers to the method of earning rent charges whereby the rent charge each month is proportional to the remaining lease balance. Under this method, the lessor or assignee earns rent charges at an equal rate over the lease term.

**Consummation**—Generally, the time at which the lessee and the lessor sign the lease agreement.

**Dealer Preparation Fee**—A fee charged by some dealers to cover the expenses of preparing a vehicle for lease.

**Default**—The lessee's failure to meet one or more conditions of the lease agreement, which may result in early termination of the lease.

**Depreciation and Amortized Amounts**—A major part of the monthly leasing payment which represents the total of (1) amount charged to cover the vehicle's projected decline in value through normal use during the lease term; and (2) other items that are paid for over the lease term, that are calculated as the difference between the adjusted capitalized cost and the vehicle's residual value.

**Disclosures**—Information on the financial terms and other terms and conditions of a lease, including information required by federal regulation (Regulation M) and by state laws, which must be given to a prospective lessee before the lease is consummated. Also refers to key lease terms that must be included in lease advertisements. Required disclosures must be made in writing before the lease is consummated.

**Disposition Fee**—Also known as a disposal fee, refers to a fee often charged by a lessor or assignee to defray the cost of preparing and selling the vehicle at the end of the lease if the lessee does not purchase the vehicle but instead returns it to the lessor or assignee.

**Documentation Fee**—Also known as a dealer documentation fee, refers to a fee charged by some dealerships or other lessors to cover the cost of preparing lease documents.

**Down Payment**—An initial cash payment in a lease that reduces the capitalized cost or is applied to other amounts due at lease signing.

**Early Termination**—Ending the lease before the scheduled termination date for any reason, voluntary or involuntary, at which time an early termination charge may apply.

**Early Termination Charge**—The amount owed if the lease ends before its scheduled termination date, calculated as described in the lease agreement, but is generally the difference between the early termination payoff and the amount credited to for the vehicle.

**Early Termination Payoff**—Also known as the early termination balance or gross payoff, refers to the total amount owed if the lease is terminated before the scheduled end of the term, before the value credited to the lessee for the vehicle is subtracted, that is calculated as described in the lease agreement, and may include the unpaid lease balance and other charges.

**Equal Credit Opportunity Act**—A federal law that prohibits discrimination in credit transactions on the basis of race, color, religion, national origin, sex, marital status, age, source of income, or the exercise of any right under the Consumer Credit Protection Act.

**Equity**—In an installment sale or loan, the positive difference between the trade-in or market value of the vehicle and the loan payoff amount.

**Excess Mileage Charge**—A charge by the lessor or assignee for miles driven in excess of the maximum specified in the lease agreement.

**Excessive Wear-and-Tear Charge**—Amount charged by a lessor or assignee to cover wear and tear on a leased vehicle beyond what is considered normal, which may cover both interior and exterior damage, such as upholstery stains, body dents and scrapes, and tire wear beyond the limits stated in the lease agreement.

**Excessive Wear-and-Tear Coverage**—A plan the lessee may purchase that covers some or all of the charges for excessive wear and tear defined in the lease agreement.

**Excessive Wear-and-Use Charge**—Sum of the excess mileage charge and the excessive wear-and-tear charge.

**Fair Market Value**—The amount that a willing buyer would pay to a willing seller to purchase certain property at a particular point in time.

**Fair-Market-Value Purchase Option**—The right to purchase a leased vehicle at scheduled termination in accordance with the terms specified in the lease agreement for a price determined by referring to a readily available guide to used-car values or another independent source.

**Federal Reserve Board**—The federal agency with rule-writing authority for the Truth in Lending Act, of which the Consumer Leasing Act is part; officially known as the Board of Governors of the Federal Reserve System.

**Federal Trade Commission**—The federal agency responsible for enforcing the Truth in Lending Act, of which the Consumer Leasing Act is part, among leasing companies, finance companies, lessors, and assignees not regulated by other federal agencies.

**Fees and Taxes**—The total amount the lessee will pay for taxes, licenses, registration fees, title fees, and official governmental fees over the term of the lease.

**Fixed-Price Purchase Option**—The right to purchase a leased vehicle at scheduled termination for a fixed price specified in the lease agreement.

**Full-Maintenance Lease**—A lease in which the lessor or assignee assumes responsibility for all manufacturer-recommended maintenance and service on the vehicle, and which may also cover additional mechanical repairs and servicing during the term of the lease, the cost of which is included in the gross capitalized cost or is added to the base monthly payment.

**GAP**—Guaranteed auto protection.

**Gap Amount**—In the event a leased vehicle is stolen or totaled, the difference between the early termination payoff amount, not including any past-due amounts, and the amount for which the vehicle is insured before the insurance deductible and any other policy deductions are subtracted.

**Gap Coverage**—A plan that provides financial protection in case the leased vehicle is stolen or totaled in an accident.

**Gross Capitalized Cost**—Also known as gross cap cost, refers to the agreed-upon value of the vehicle at the time it is leased, plus any items the lessee agrees to pay for over the lease term, such as taxes, fees, service contracts, insurance, and any prior credit or lease balance.

**Incentives**—Amounts rebated or credited, or special programs offered to encourage the leasing of certain vehicles.

**Independent Leasing Company**—A leasing company that offers leases directly to consumers and businesses and is generally not affiliated with a particular automobile manufacturer.

**Insurance**—A contract in which one party agrees to pay for another party's financial loss resulting from a specified event, such as a collision.

**Insurance Verification**—The process of obtaining verbal or written confirmation of required coverage from the lessee's insurance agent or company.

**Late Charge**—A fee charged for a past-due payment. This charge is usually either a percentage of the lease payment or a fixed dollar amount.

**Late Payment**—A payment received after the specified due date, usually made after the grace period.

**Lease**—A contract between a lessor and a lessee for the use of a vehicle or other property, subject to stated terms and limitations, for a specified period and at a specified payment.

**Lease Balance**—Also known as the adjusted lease balance, refers to the unpaid portion of the adjusted capitalized cost of the lease, which is reduced as the lease payments are made.

**Lease Extension**—Continuation of a lease agreement beyond the original term, often 1 month at a time.

**Lease Payments**—The number of payments in the lease agreement.

**Lease Rate**—A percentage used by some lessors or assignees to describe the rent charge portion of the monthly payment.

**Lease Term**—The period of time for which a lease agreement is written.

**Lemon laws**—State laws that provide remedies to consumers for vehicles that repeatedly fail to meet certain standards of quality and performance.

**Lessee**—The party to whom the vehicle is leased, e.g., the consumer in a consumer lease, who is required to make payments and meet other obligations specified in the lease agreement.

**Lessor**—A person or organization that regularly leases, offers to lease, or arranges for the lease of a vehicle.

**Maintenance**—Care for the vehicle required by the lease agreement that may include manufacturer-recommended servicing and any repairs needed to keep the vehicle in good operating condition.

**Maintenance Contract**—A contract that the lessee may purchase to cover some or all of the vehicle maintenance and servicing.

**Maintenance Lease**—A lease agreement in which some or all of the vehicle maintenance and servicing is the responsibility of the lessor or assignee.

**Mileage Allowance**—Also known as the mileage limitation, refers to the fixed mileage limit for the lease term, which, if exceeded, may result in an excess mileage charge.

**Model Lease Forms**—Sample disclosure forms developed by the Federal Reserve Board.

**Money Factor**—Also known as a lease factor, refers to a number, often given as a decimal, used by some lessors or assignees to determine the rent charge portion of the monthly payment.

**Monthly Sales/Use Taxes**—The state and local taxes that the lessee must pay monthly when they lease a vehicle which are added to the lessee's base monthly payment and paid as part of the total monthly payment.

**Manufacturer's Suggested Retail Price (MSRP)**—The sticker price for the vehicle.

**Nonsegregated Disclosures**—Disclosures required by Federal Reserve Board Regulation M that may be presented in any order and may appear anywhere in the lease documents except with the segregated disclosures.

**Open-End Lease**—A lease agreement in which the amount owed at the end of the lease term is based on the difference between the residual value of the leased property and its realized value.

**Personal Property**—Any property that is not real property under the law of the state where the property is located at the time it is offered or made available for lease.

**Personal Property Tax**—Also known as ad valorem tax, refers to a tax on personal property.

**Prior Credit Balance**—Also known as negative equity or negative trade-in balance, refers to the portion of the gross capitalized cost representing the amount due under a previous credit contract after the value of the vehicle traded in on the lease has been credited.

**Prior Lease Balance**—The portion of the gross capitalized cost representing the balance due under a previous lease agreement after the value of the previously leased vehicle has been credited.

**Purchase Option**—The lessee's right to buy the vehicle they have leased, before or at the end of the lease term, according to terms specified in the lease agreement.

**Purchase-Option Fee**—An amount, in addition to the purchase price, the lessee may have to pay to exercise any purchase option in the lease agreement.

**Realized Value**—(1) The amount received by the lessor or assignee for the leased vehicle at disposition; (2) the highest offer for the leased vehicle at disposition; or (3) the fair market value of the leased vehicle at termination.

**Reasonableness Standard**—The requirement of the Consumer Leasing Act that charges for delinquency, default, or early termination be reasonable in light of the lessor's or assignee's (1) anticipated or actual harm caused by such delinquency, default, or early termination, (2) difficulties in proving loss, and (3) inconvenience in obtaining a remedy.

**Rebate**—An amount that may be offered by a manufacturer, dealer, lessor, or assignee that may be paid to the lessee separately or credited to their lease agreement.

**Reconditioning**—The process of preparing a vehicle for resale or re-lease if it is returned.

**Reconditioning Reserve**—An amount the lessee may pay at the beginning of the lease that may be used by the lessor or assignee to offset any amounts the lessee may owe at the end of the lease term for excessive wear and use and excess mileage

**Registration Fee**—A fee charged by a state motor vehicle department to register a vehicle and authorize its use on the public roadways.

**Regulation M**—The regulation issued by the Federal Reserve that implements the Consumer Leasing Act.

**Rent**—Also known as the rent charge, refers to the portion of the lessee's base monthly payment that is not depreciation or any amortized amounts.

**Residual Value**—The end-of-term value of the vehicle established at the beginning of the lease and used in calculating the lessee's base monthly payment.

**Residual Value Guidebooks**—Publications used, in part, by some lessors and assignees to establish vehicle residual values.

**Sales/Use Taxes**—Taxes assessed on leased and purchased vehicles.

**Security Deposit**—An amount the lessee may be required to pay, usually at the beginning of the lease, that may be used by the lessor or assignee in the event of default or at the end of the lease to offset any amounts the lessee may owe under the lease agreement.

**Security Interest**—If stated in the lease agreement, refers to a lessor's or assignee's legal right to the property that secures payment of the lessee's obligation under the lease agreement.

**Segregated Disclosures**—Disclosures required by Federal Reserve Board Regulation M that must be grouped together and separated from other information in the lease documents.

**Service Contract**—Also known as mechanical breakdown coverage or an extended warranty, refers to a contract the lessee may purchase to cover such expenses as the repair or replacement of vehicle components and, in some cases, related services such as towing or replacement rental cars.

**Single-Payment Lease**—A lease that requires a single payment made in advance rather than periodic payments made over the term of the lease.

**Standards for Wear and Use**—Statements in the lease agreement defining what the lessor or assignee means by normal wear and use and setting the requirements for the vehicle's condition at the end of the lease.

**Sublease**—Oral or written contractual transfer of the leased vehicle to another person that generally requires the lessor's or assignee's approval.

**Subvention**—A program or plan in which certain items are subsidized by the manufacturer, the finance company, the lessor, or the assignee.

**Time Value of Money**—The value derived from the use of money over time as a result of investment and reinvestment.

**Title**—Legal document that identifies the owner of the vehicle.

**Total Contractual Obligation**—The sum of the capitalized cost reduction, the total of base monthly payments, and other charges due under the lease agreement, excluding any security deposit, sales taxes and any other fees and taxes paid to a third party.

**Total Monthly Payment**—The base monthly payment plus monthly sales or use taxes and any other monthly charges.

**Total of Payments**—The sum of the periodic payments, the end-of-term disposition fee, any other charges, and all amounts due at lease signing or delivery, minus refundable amounts such as a security deposit and any monthly payments included in the amount due at lease signing or delivery.

**Trade-in**—The net value of a vehicle credited toward the purchase or lease of another vehicle

**Used-Car Guidebooks**—Publications that report current wholesale and/or retail prices of used vehicles.

**Used-Vehicle Leasing**—Leasing of previously driven owned or leased vehicles.

**Warranty**—A guarantee that the vehicle will function and perform as specified, and covering specified mechanical problems for a fixed period of time or number of miles.

# BIBLIOGRAPHY AND ADDITIONAL RESOURCES

*Black's Law Dictionary, Fifth Edition*. St. Paul, MN: West Publishing Company, 1979.

Consumer Action (Date Visited: September 2005) <http://www. consumer-action. org/>.

National Automobile Dealer Association (Date Visited: September 2005) <http://www.nada.org/>.

National Vehicle Leasing Association (Dated Visited: September 2005) <http://www.nvla.org/>.

The Federal Reserve Board (Date Visited: September 2005) <http://www.federalreserve.gov/>.

The Federal Trade Commission (Date Visited: September 2005) <http://www.ftc.gov/>.